The Message from the All
The Prophecy of God Today – Not the Word of the Bible

Volume 1

The Message from the All

The Prophecy of God Today – Not the Word of the Bible

Volume 1

THE WORD
THE UNIVERSAL SPIRIT

First Edition, 2009
Published by:
© Universal Life
The Inner Religion
PO Box 3549
Woodbridge, CT 06525
U S A

Licensed edition
translated from the original German title:
Die Botschaft aus dem All
Die Gottes Prophetie Heute
Nicht das Bibelwort, Band 1
Order No. S 137en

From the Universal Life Series
with the consent of
© Verlag DAS WORT GmbH
im Universellen Leben
Max-Braun-Str. 2
97828 Marktheidenfeld/Altfeld, Germany

The German edition is the work of reference for all
questions regarding the meaning of the contents

All rights reserved

ISBN 978-1-890841-36-2

Table of Contents

Introduction	7
I AM, and You Are in Me, Infinitely Eternal – and You Return Through Christ	13
You Spurn the One God – and Believe in Eternal Damnation. I Am the God of Love! The Earth Calls to Me, the Creator, for Mercy	31
The One Who Knows Me Walks at My Hand	49
Are You Servile to the God of the Underworld and His Idols?	58
I Make All Things New	75
When the Hour Strikes	91
Let It Become As It Is In Heaven!	104
Do You Speak the Language of Love?	113
The World Talks About Peace. Where Is the Peace?	121
Where Do You Stand? At My Right Hand?	133
Are You True Christians In My Following?	143

Do You Want to Be My Disciple? 154

Feel ME Present in You 166

God Breathes Back the Fall.
The True Life Opens Up 176

Books in the Universal Life Series 189

The Message From the All
The Prophecy of God Today
Not the Word of the Bible
VOLUME 1

Introduction

Through His mission, Jesus of Nazareth has called into being an inner religion. However, the growing externalization of Christianity has again caused a growing rigidity of religious life, isolating itself from the true Original Christian stream, which now has reached its lowest point – 2000 years after the Christ of God's journey over the earth. Moreover, the cyclical irradiation from the central cosmic primordial star, the Primordial Central Sun, has indicated the repatriation of the fallen ones. And so, a great prophet has once again come to mankind by order of the Eternal One.

It is now a female being, a woman, Gabriele, the teaching prophetess and messenger of God for this our time – a time in which a mighty radical change and spiritual departure are imminent, the greatest turn of time within living memory.

By way of the instrument of God, the cherub of divine Wisdom, called Brother Emanuel for us human beings, said the following in a revelation at the Table of the Lord in 1998:

It is high time for mankind to understand that in this mighty turn of time the eternal Spirit, GOD, opened the heavens very wide and sent a prophet, a prophetess, who brought to the people the eternal word of love, of truth and of peace.

Verily, I say to you: Jesus, the Christ, was the greatest prophet. But after Jesus, the Christ, the instrument through which I am speaking is the greatest prophet. Never before was heaven so wide open as during this earthly time ...

The All-Spirit, God, the Spirit of the Christ of God, gave and gives to us human beings His mighty word through Gabriele. Our physical ears may hear what our spiritual ears are no longer able to perceive: God's message to us.

In countless revelations, God-Father, Christ and other spirit beings give us an understanding of what we need to again recognize ourselves as those who we have been from the very beginning, so that we are able to grasp our personal situation as well as the state of mankind and of the planet Earth and – with the redeeming, liberating and guiding power of Christ, who took up dwelling in every heart – are able to set out again on the way home to the inner Kingdom of God.

Two thousand years ago, Jesus of Nazareth said: *I have yet many things to say to you, but you cannot bear them now. When the Spirit of truth comes, he will guide you into all the truth.* (Jo. 16:12) This has been taking place through Gabriele. In the prophetic word, she passes on the all-encompassing language of light of the eternal Spirit in our human language, in a depth, clarity, conciseness and richness that is unique in the history of mankind. Since Gabriele's spiritual consciousness is fully developed, that is, since she lives in the consciousness of God, she draws directly from the eternal stream and offers us human beings the whole truth.

The fourteen great divine revelations selected for this volume – revelations given by God-Father and by the Christ of God from the years 1987 to 1998 – and thus published in written form for the first time, were broadcast in worldwide transmissions and by way of radio in the series *The All-Spirit, GOD, Speaks Directly into Our Time through His Prophetess . He Does Not Speak the Word of the Bible.*

These revelations are a gift from God, the All-Spirit, to all people who accept Him in His word and who want to allow what is given in it to become effective in their life.

God gives, and gives in fullness. God offers us His truth, His light, His strength, His explanations and guidance, His love. He does not want us to suffer and vegetate in misery and affliction. But we – every single one of us – are free to decide for ourselves whether we want to accept or not that which flows from His caring heart for us. Here, too, His word holds true: *May the one who can grasp it, grasp it. May the one who wants to leave it, leave it.*

The Message from the All
The Prophecy of God Today – Not the Word of the Bible

Volume 1

I AM,
and You Are in Me, Infinitely Eternal – and You Return Through Christ

God-Father Revelation, 1990

God-Father:
Infinite eternity – Infinite eternity streams through the universe, through space and time. Infinite eternity is the law of eternal love, the I Am from eternity to eternity.

Infinite eternity – so it streams through you, too, My child. Infinite eternity is the spirit of love and of life, Am I, the All-stream – for you, for all Being.

Oh see, out of Myself, the All-stream, I manifested Myself and became your Father – for out of one and the same stream, which I Am, I created you, too. I also manifested you by way of spiritual procreation, through the life that I Am.

My child, you are now in an earthly garment – but what is the mere external manifestation, the outer shell, when your inner being is in the light of truth?

My child, do you stand in the light of truth? Then, the Redeemer-spark has become one with Me, the Pri-

mordial Light, and you are again consciously the son and the daughter of Mine, of your Father. But as long as you live in the illusory images of matter, you turn away again and again from the inner light, from Me. This is why many a person cannot grasp that I, the Eternal, speak to My own.

My child, whether you are doubtful or unbelieving – I speak! For I Am the speaking God deep in your soul. I Am the speaking God in all suns and stars; I Am the speaking God in every plant, in every stone, in every animal. I Am the speaking God in every drop of water, in every radiation of the stars. I Am infinity, the cosmos – and you, My child, bear as essence in you the whole of infinity, all Being, in the very depths of your soul.

My child, recognize the depths of your inner life, and feel Me in you! Become aware that you are never lonely and alone! The primordial power and the Christ-power are active in you and irradiate you untiringly. Know, My child, that you are embedded in the mighty All that is your eternal homeland – for you are a child of infinity, a child of the All.

See, when I envisioned you, created you – and placed you in the heavenly planes as a being of light – I also breathed freedom into you. To be free means to live the law of love, the All-law. Whoever lives the law of love, *the All-law, also has absolute freedom of movement in all of infinity. Nothing is unfamiliar to a pure being. A pure being can make use of every radiation of infinity, because every radiation is active in him, and therefore perfect.*

Through the Fall, through the burdening of the soul, the spirit being limited itself more and more; its radiation decreased and it turned to self-will, wanting to be more than God – to be equal to Him, in order to then be above Him.

In this way, the burdened souls created their own law; you call it the law of sowing and reaping. Whoever lives under this law of sowing and reaping is sinful; and the more he sins, the more he turns away from the eternal law, from the All-law of love – and thus, from Me, his Father.

The Father, who I Am, then becomes foreign to him. It is a remote God, possibly even a God of punishment and chastisement – for your own causes become active and you attribute them to Me. Because of this, fear, hatred, discord and much more came into being.

Many of My children sinned more and more. They wove themselves more and more into the law of sowing and reaping. They fell further and further and turned away from the inner light. The love, which I Am, went after them through the prophets. I spoke at all times through the mouths of prophets, because many of My own, who had woven themselves into the law of sowing and reaping, could no longer understand or even hear Me.

It is similar at this earthly time, in your generation. If My own would walk the path to the inner light, if they would become aware of their origin, they would then recognize and feel Me, their eternal Father, and would live consciously in the All-law of love and life.

Oh recognize: As long as people continue to turn away from Me, I will call them – and My Son, who became your Redeemer, will also do this. Yes, He became your Redeemer! Are you aware of this? Are you aware of what Jesus of Nazareth took on Himself? You simply say: "The sins of this world" – He took on Himself the disobedience of many people, the disobedience of the lineage of David, and the disobedience of other lineages, the disobedience of the Jews. For many who were in the earthly garment with Him had made a promise in the eternal Jerusalem, and made an avowal of unity and brotherhood with Him for all the earth, for all the world.

My Son came; but sin lay over His own and blinded their eyes. They looked only at the deception, at illusion and trivialities and did not recognize the simplicity of the great Spirit in Jesus of Nazareth. So that His own might awaken to the great task of Redemption in the Spirit of love, He enveloped Himself with several unlawful forces, primarily, a part of the guilt of the lineage of David. In this way, He became visible for the darkness. They took Him captive, led Him before the court and accused Him of sin. But I say to you: My Son was without flaw. He served only the law of love and His neighbor.

And, in a similar way He served on Calvary, too. He served while they nailed Him to the cross and raised Him high. He served the people; He served the lineage of David which promised to become active for the great totality. He served the Jews, among whom were many from other tribes, who were also a part of the mission. He served so that they recognize their causes more quickly, in order to clear them up and then be available for the great plan of leading all back, of leading all home to the eternal Father-house.

My children, what happened? Through the blindness of many people, Jesus of Nazareth has been derided and mocked right up until the present generation. What does the cross mean to you? For some people, does it represent the downfall of Jesus of Nazareth? Then they worship the corpus. Does it represent the resurrection for you? In this case, you look only to the cross of redemption – without the corpus. For the cross of redemption is the cross of victory – in Christ, for Christ and with Christ. Whoever looks up to the corpus, to the crucified One on the cross, has eyes that have been dulled by sin and thus pays homage to the darkness, which has placed the body on its banner symbolizing the downfall of the Nazarene.

Oh recognize, the earthly body was taken down from the cross, because the "It is finished" had been spoken; the Redeemer-spark entered the souls – but the wholly spiritualized earthly body was brought into even more vibration by Me and transformed into higher substances.

My children, not a single speck of dust from His earthly body remains on this earth – everything was transformed into the primordial substance, because the "It is finished" was spoken from the purity of His body.

But what did the darkness do? Again it made use of sinful people who were – and are – blinded by vain illusion, who took the cross with the corpus and continue to set it up again and again. Thus, they want to symbolize that Jesus was defeated by His sins and that the power of darkness prevails.

Verily, I say to you: When you worship the corpus on the cross in this way and beseech Jesus on the cross, then you are giving part of the power of your prayer to the darkness – for the corpus on the cross is the banner of the darkness. In this way, My Son was and is derided and mocked; and the blind who live in sin and maintain and increase their sins do not recognize the difference between the cross with the corpus, the dead body, and the cross without the corpus.

The cross is the sign of redemption; it is the sign of the resurrection. And when My children resurrect in Christ, they carry the cross of victory over themselves, for the cross without the corpus is the cross of redemption and the cross of resurrection.

Have you resurrected, My child? You have redemption in you. Have you resurrected in Christ, by endeavoring to follow Him every day, to keep the laws of inner life and of selfless love? If not, then you are suppressing the light of redemption, reducing it to a tiny glow, and you continue to pay homage to sinfulness – and to all those who are in sin.

Christ was and is derided and mocked. Many mourn before the cross with the corpus. It would be better if they would mourn for themselves and in their mourning recognize their sins, with which they daily crucify Christ, the inner life. In the end, they thus impose upon themselves the burden of the cross with the corpus, for they do not pay homage to the risen Christ, but to the dead one.

My children, how long do you want to live with these illusions? How long will you continue to be kept prisoner by sin, your eyes dulled? How long do you want to carry on under the slavery of your own ego – how long? Christ, the inner life, your Redeemer, is spanned before your political parties like a horse before a wagon, and its purpose is to draw in and win over those who blindly listen to them, simply because the word "Christ" or "Christian" is standing at the front of the wagon.

How long do you want to remain blind and crucify your brother and Redeemer? How long? And it is said: "You will be saved through faith alone." If this were so, the world would be whole, and all people would be saved. Faith is the first step toward the inner light – trust is the next step. And it is a tremendous step when you entrust yourself to Christ, your Redeemer – in that you strive to sin less and less, in that you strive to keep peace with your neighbor, in that you strive to forgive, to ask for forgiveness, and to sin no more.

Then you experience the resurrection in yourself, because the Redeemer-light in your soul becomes ever greater. Your consciousness expands; sin falls from your eyes; and you see more clearly and see, too, how Christ is derided and mocked. You will not become a seeing person through faith alone! The law of love enables you to see – and whosoever truly wants to see shall fulfill the law of love, and he will then enter the inner life.

Oh recognize, My children, the Spirit will continue to speak to you until you are largely free from sin, so that you may then turn into the stream, the infinite eternity, so that you may speak with Me face to face, *just as you spoke when you were with Me in the Sanctum as pure children of love.*

Christ leads you back again – Christ alone, My Son, the Co-Regent of the heavens! And even though you follow ever so many ostensible christs – no matter whether they are spanned before a wagon or whether they belong to denominations – I say to you: The Christ of the inner being is the true Christ, and no human being can lead you to Me – other than the Christ who is in you. He announced the laws of salvation to you as Jesus of Nazareth; He announces the laws of inner life to you once again. The one who accepts them finds his way to the inner Christ, and attains the resurrection in Christ, and in Me, his Father.

My child, how long do you still want to pay tribute to sin? How long do you want to walk over this earth – blind, suffering, ill and infirm? How long? How long will you continue to seek in the outer world for people who might possibly be able to show you the path to Christ? Oh see, people can walk the path to Christ and, from their actualization, pass on to you what they have explored and experienced, and still experience, in the very depths of their soul. But you have to start with yourself, and the help is Christ in you, the redeeming power.

My child, how long do you want to pay homage to the Demons' State, by sinning more and more? How long will you continue to live in the illusion that faith alone is supposed to save you? Believe in the inner power; entrust yourself to Christ, and walk the path of spiritualization by recognizing your sins, surrendering them to Christ and sinning no more. This is the path – and there is no other way! No matter how many paths are offered on this earth, no matter what is read from your Bibles – a person who does not actualize it is a fool and remains a sinner who is kept blind, blindly doing what others tell him to.

My children, I do not bind you to My word, either. I have spoken to you and will continue to speak. I Am your Father and, in the stream of life, I Am the Father-Mother-God, who envelops you and leads you through Christ. Whether you want to believe it or not is a matter for your own judgment. I, the pure life, do not influence My children, but many of My children are under the influence of the darkness and allow all that is against Me to flow into them.

Receive the sign of Redemption into yourself! In the midst of this place, the radiating cross comes down. My Son stands in your midst. Through the radiating cross without the corpus, He symbolizes the resurrection and the life. In your midst, He raises His arms, opens them wide, calling out: "Oh come all of you to Me, all those who are weary and heavy-laden – and I will quicken you!"

Where shall you go? Solely within! For there, deep in your inner being, in your soul, yes, in every cell of your body, is the power of liberation, the redemption; it is Christ, the light.

Go within and feel in every cell of your body the radiating cross, the cross of redemption and resurrection. And if you are consciously resurrected ones, you see the mighty radiating cross in your midst. And if you can perceive it in your inner being, you will be touched by some of its rays.

What do you want to do with your Redeemer? He is calling: "Come all of you to Me, all who are weary and heavy-laden – and I will quicken you." Yes, He left the eternal Being, became human and returned as a pure being. However, He left His power, His light, the Redemption, with you, in you, in each and every soul. But how deceptive are all outer forms, dogmas and rites – all external splendor and glitter! You will continue to need all of this until you have become the inner radiance again. However, when you look only at outer trivia, how can you attain inner radiance, the light of salvation, peace, love, your infinite, eternal heritage, because you are immortal?

My child, whether you believe it or not: Salvation is in you, and only in you! Everything external, all rituals and forms, all kinds of showy splendor, are not a part of your nature. In you is the light, and when you have become the light of love, then you will recognize that the heavens within you are open, and that the radiance of the heavens is your true being, the intensity of your radiation. If a soul has lost this inner radiance, then it seeks external baubles, outer brightness, and hangs on to honors and titles and holds on to means and money, because, deep within, it is impoverished.

My child! You are My child; become aware of this and take the radiating cross into your consciousness. Absorb the words and grasp the meaning of "Christ": "Come here, My child! No matter what you bear, be it sin or light – I love you. Come here; I want to help you; I want to edify and quicken you! Come here!" This is what Christ is saying every moment in you, My child; for His striving is to lead you to Me – home, home into the eternal, boundless infinity. Home through Christ. Home, in that you, My child, open up the inner kingdom, in that you cause your soul to shine, so that it may feel the breath of infinity and bear the radiating crown of inner love – the law of infinity.

My child, come home! You are not lost. When sad or bleak hours come, then remember: Christ is calling in you. When joyful hours come, do not forget the inner love! Give thanks for the joyful hours and days, give thanks – then joy will also flow from your heart and you will see what resurrection means. Then your prayers will become selfless, because you yourself become ever more selfless. Then your inner being will become filled with light and power and will unite more and more with the stream of inner life, that I Am.

And so, what do you want to do with Christ? What do you want to do with your earthly life? What do you want to do with your five senses? Do you want to refine them, or do you want them to continue being kept blind?

My child, the love, which I Am in Christ, is always present. And the one who prays from his heart and fulfills his prayers, who clears up every single day what the day brings him, attains resurrection already in the earthly body, and the union, the becoming and being one, with Me, the primordial light.

My child, Christ wants to guide you out of the bleak hours, yes, also out of the bleak days and years that this earth, this world, will experience. This is why He speaks untiringly, also through the prophetic word, so that your external ears can hear Him, for He wants to make you free from sin, free from compulsion and conceptions. He wants to make you seeing, so that you see the blind leaders of the blind, who lead people astray in the name of the cross, and in the name of Christ.

I say to you: Listen only to the law of love! It is given to you in the commandments; it is given to you through *the Inner Path; it is given to you in the many words and explanations. You, do not cling to the word that you have read or heard! What you can accept – this, My child, you should actualize! Then your consciousness will expand and you will recognize that the guidance takes place from within, from your Redeemer, Christ. Then there will no longer be a need for outer leaders; you will see through them, the blind leaders of the blind. And the cross of redemption will change – and in you, your being will show itself pure, noble and beautiful. The redemption is completed; you are resurrected in Christ. Christ will then consciously be your brother, and the messengers of heaven will consciously be your brothers and sisters. Your eyes will see all people and beings – and in them you will likewise recognize your brothers and sisters, because you bear them within you. This is the life of unity. In the life of unity there is no above and below, no in front and behind, no right and no left. Nor is there the woman as a woman, the man as a man; both are one in Christ, as brother and sister, and live in purity and beget in purity and receive, in turn, the life, in purity.*

This is the path of inner life; this is your path. As long as you separate, you do not experience what unity means; you do not experience what peace and love mean; you speak about it – and do not experience it. As long as there is no peace in your marriages – also called families and partnerships – you are against the law of

All-harmony; you are against the law of duality. For what is in heaven shall also be on earth: two people, woman and man, united in love for neighbor; woman and man in the great family of God – One for all and all for One. As long as this is not so, you are blind and against the inner life, because you are against your neighbor.

The duality in the eternal Being is a sacred bond for all eternity. And your marriages, also your partnerships – no matter what you call them – should be a sacred covenant with Me, in that you clear up with one another what brought you together, so that you may consciously become brothers and sisters in the light of truth, and so that your children may become children of the Father-Mother-God, because you are good examples for them. All this is a part of the cross of redemption and of the resurrection in Christ.

Just as above, will it become similar on earth. My Son went out for this and many with Him. The materialistic world is fading; the effects are taking their course, the earth is in revolt, but salvation is here: Christ, the Savior!

My children, do not ask where Christ is! Do not seek Him here and there. Go into your inner being, Christ is there. You will become aware of Him, if you rid yourself of your sins one by one, through His help and with His power.

Oh see, I Am the Spirit of freedom – I leave you the freedom. Each one can decide: for the inner light, or for external appearances.

But recognize, My children, your true inner being is immortal, just as I Am immortal and invincible. No matter what the darkness is able to accomplish with the name "Christ" – Christ is the victor! He, in Me, and I, in Him, are invincible. The sign of the cross without the corpus is the sign of redemption, of resurrection; it is the sign that points the way to the eternal light.

Whatever you think, however you act – you have free will. But one day you will come to realize that you are immortal! Then so-called death will be overcome; you will take off the shell and return to the Father-house, because you have opened up the inner kingdom.

Recognize: Death is overcome in Christ. But the person who does not live in Christ suffers and fears so-called death, because he, himself, is still spiritually dead and spiritually blind.

My children, infinite eternity – infinite eternity streams through infinity, through space and time! Infinite eternity floods through you, too, My child, because you are in Me, eternally. No matter what you think, no matter what you do, whether you accept or reject Christ, whether you doubt Me or affirm Me – My child, you are in Me, your Father, and I see you, eternally, just as I created you and placed you into the heavenly planes: pure, eternally young, beautiful, the radiating law of love! This, My child, is what you are in Me. And this is how you will return to Me. And with your pure eyes, you will look into My pure eyes, into My countenance. And we will meet each other in our inner being, as though you had never been away from Me. For you are always in Me; no matter where you are, no matter what path you take – you are in Me!

And when you return, you will recognize the fusion. It was and is always just as I have envisioned, created and made you, and you experience that there was and is no separation. We are united, My child; we are united – I keep you in the stream of My heart. We are united, infinitely eternally, My child, infinitely eternally, from eternity to eternity. This is your Father, given in words through My instrument. For when you look into the words, you grasp My love and you realize that I have very personally addressed you, you, you, every single one of you. I know you. I have called you by your eternal name that is given to you infinitely eternally – infinitely eternally, My child!

I Am and you are in Me, and you will return through Christ.

My child, do not cause yourself pain by sinning! My child, do not cause yourself suffering and worry by sinning! My child, do not inflict illness upon your-

self by sinning. Recognize yourself; go to Christ, clear things up, and you will experience the conscious resurrection in Christ.

I Am, and you are! Even when My words through the mouth of a prophet fade away – I Am, and you are. And My voice is the All in all things – deep in your neighbor, deep in you, in the stars, in the nature kingdoms, in the minerals and in the stones, everywhere, in every atom: I Am. I Am near you, My child; you and I are the eternity.

I Am, and you are from eternity to eternity, My child, I, your eternal Father.

*You Spurn the One God –
and Believe in Eternal Damnation.
I Am the God of Love!
The Earth Calls to Me, the Creator,
for Mercy*

God-Father Revelation, 1996

I AM the God of Abraham, the God of Isaac and the God of Jacob. I AM the God of all true prophets. I Am the God of the heavens and of this earth. I AM not the God of this world.

Through the mouth of a prophet I, the God of the heavens, speak into this world, so that those people can understand Me who still think that as human beings they are My children. But I say to you: My child is the innermost part in your souls, in the very basis of the soul. This is from My heart; this remains in My heart, and this will also return to My heart.

Many a person asks himself: "Why did the Fall take place?" But I say the following to you: With the act of creation, with the first segment of creation, I created children from the eternal stream, the stream of the Father-Mother-Being, the stream of life, of one power and one source, which I, the God of the heavens, Am. Verily, as this segment perfected itself more and more, as the first basic heavens opened up, one being wanted to be like Me. It wanted the heart to be divided – into God and Goddess. But I did not allow this – for it is **one** stream; it is **one** source eternally – and out of this one source I created My children and I created them, the children of the heavens, so that they became heirs to the totality and so that all those who emerge from the principle of duality again become heirs to the totality. If I had divided My heart, I would have divided the universe for the Goddess and for the God, and My children would have been part heirs. My being is the totality. My stream is one stream, the source of life for all My children, for all animals, plants and minerals. And thus, I, the Father-Mother-God, the one source, created My children from the one stream of the one source and they became heirs to the totality. From this one source, the principle of duality also flowed out. This means: two and yet **one** heart, that complements itself in giving and receiving. From this principle of giving and receiving, from the one heart of the principle of duality, further children of the heavens emerge; they are, in turn, heirs to the totality, that is, heirs to the eternal Being. If I had divided creation, then it would be similar as in this your world, which consists of "divide, bind and rule."

Verily, the Fall is merely a turbulence in the final stage of fermentation. And when My children have fully *fermented, they will return to the One who envisioned and created them. Spoken with your words, that was and is the Fall. Many beings joined the one being and fell. Others went out to instruct the Fall-beings and fell away from Me; these are then the fallen ones. Many of them are romping about on this earth and call their dwelling places their world.*

Verily, I say to you: This world is not My world. It belongs to the Fall and to the god of the underworld. The one who serves the god of the underworld destroys the earth and creates his own primitive world out of the destruction of the earth.

Look into the world of your thoughts. Whom do you pay homage to – the God of the heavens or the god of the underworld? The god of the underworld wants this world in which you live. But I, the God of the heavens, want to lead you into the worlds of the eternal Being through My Son, your Redeemer – whom you do not receive in your hearts because you do not do what He, as Jesus of Nazareth, taught you and lived for you as an example. And so, many of you belong to the god of the underworld and serve his gods.

Verily, verily, I say to you: Your feelings, sensations, thoughts, words and deeds tell you whom you serve! Do not flatter your habitus, by believing that you are Christians. I say to you, that your gods, who serve the god of the underworld, have led you away from the

God of the heavens. They talk about a god who punishes, who chastises, who damns you, yes, who casts you into eternal damnation. But I say to you: That is the god of the underworld, not the God of the heavens, who I Am. I Am the God of love, of whom My Son spoke as Jesus of Nazareth.

You people are so proud of your intellect. Switch it on for a short moment and consider: If I were the god of the Old Testament, then Jesus of Nazareth would have taught wrongly, for He taught you about another God: the God of love, the God of peace, the God of unity, the God of mercy, of forgiveness, and never the god of punishment! Who spoke rightly: the god of the underworld, who sneaked into the Old Testament and also into the statements of the prophets – which means they were translated incorrectly – or was Jesus, the Christ, your Redeemer, a false prophet? One must have been right – the god of the Old Testament or the God in Jesus, the Christ.

*Verily, verily, I say to you that Jesus, the Christ, the greatest prophet of all time, your Redeemer, spoke the truth, because He came to you and was and is one with Me, the God of love. Whom do **you** follow: your gods, who serve the god of the underworld?*

Oh recognize: Who called for theologians? The god of the underworld or the God of the heavens? I have none who serve Me professionally, but I do have called ones. But your servants, who crown their habitus with various headgear, no matter what you call them, do not serve Me; and they do not serve you, either – they serve themselves and thus, the one who called them. He is the one you pay homage to; these are the gods you pay homage to. You spurn the one God and believe in eternal damnation. You people of this world, is the condition you are living in not yet enough for you? Is this not already hell? Do you still want more hell or more purgatory? Are your diseases, your miseries, your worries not yet enough?

Verily, verily, I say to you: I call My children, and I call into the very basis of the people's souls. The habitus cannot understand me. The divided heart will not accept and receive Me, either. But a heart that beats entirely for Me will understand Me, the sun God, the primordial God of the eternal Being of the heavens.

Many hearts are divided. They have divided themselves into "mine" and "thine." They created and create borders and fences and think this is their small kingdom. The rich ones adorn themselves with wealth, with the corresponding energy, which you call dollars. They display themselves and shine as the "rich ones." And you – you are the imitators. Do you not know that the rich have to shine with their energies, because they are the most wretched, the poorest among the poor? This *is why they have to adorn themselves with clothing, crowns and different headgear, however you call them.*

Go into your stone houses of God – what do you see? Adorned servants. Whom do they serve? Do they serve you? Then they would not be adorned! Do they serve Me? Then they would be the least among you. But they serve the one who wants to be like Me – and he will never be able to do this, because the earth is Mine, and the earth will open up and devour everything. But your souls will keep on living in deep disgrace in the spheres of purification, which mankind created through its inputs.

Verily, verily, I say to you: I Am also the plaintiff for this earth, for the innocent creatures, for all life forms, for the animals, plants and minerals. You, who in many cases are cruelty personified, what are you doing to your divine heritage? For, taken as energy, animals, plants and stones are a part of your divine body, just as you, viewed as energy, are also a part of them. What are you doing to the animals, which I want to call your second neighbors?

Look into the barns and see how they must live, crammed into the most confining spaces. Look at their food. What is given to them? That which the flesh needs so that cannibalism begins to flourish and produces more and more infertile fruit, which is what you are! If you were crammed into spaces like the animals, then you would accuse God. Verily, I say to you: Complain to the god of the underworld, whom you frequently serve and who wants it this way.

Look into the different trucks, as you call them. Hour after hour, in terms of your time, animals are transported from one place to another. They are hungry; they suffer; they die. If you were herded together and pressed into trucks, you would accuse God. Accuse the god of your underworld, whom you have served and continue to serve.

Look into your slaughterhouses. A shot! A blow! Dead! The body torn apart with sharp knives and objects. One little animal after the other, and those who are still standing have to look on at how others of their species are slaughtered and butchered. Being afraid of what will also happen to them, of what awaits them, they scream and lament and complain and call to God, who I AM, to their Creator, for redemption. How do you redeem them? By slaughtering them in your slaughterhouses, in the woods and fields. A shot! Dead! Their body torn apart, the intestines torn out, the meat nicely prepared and cannibalism flourishes. You may not consume the flesh of your neighbor – you consume the dead flesh of your second neighbor. You are animal cannibals!

How do you still want to become children of God? Look at your fields. Artificial fertilizers, pesticides and herbicides – I use your words. You torment and maltreat your fields. When the earth gives it back to you and you become ill, you accuse God. Complain to the god of the underworld. He wants it this way, and in the end, you do, too, for you serve him.

The earth calls to Me, the Creator, for mercy, for freedom. And what do you do? You accuse Me – but complain to the one whom you serve and whom you let inspire you.

Explosives are put into the earth and then set off. Explosives in the oceans, and then ignited! Look into what happens: The heads are blown off of the animals in and on the earth and also in the air; their limbs are torn off; their lungs burst; their hearts are ripped apart; the whole body is torn into shreds. This is what you are – you let this happen! When it happens to you, you accuse Me. Accuse the one whom you serve! Swallow explosives yourself and let another set them off. What happens then? The earth-body, the Mother Earth, is large; it nourishes mankind. You think that when this or that is done in this or that place, then nothing so terrible or so much will happen to the earth, which is, as you say, a huge mass.

Verily, verily, I say to you: The vibrations of your negative behavior draw through the whole earth; they go into the atmosphere and come back to you. Who destroys the atmosphere – the God of love, who gave *the earth a mantle so that you could live on the earth? But you, every one of you, contribute to the fact that the mantle is opening up and the forces of the All are gradually burning you up. Then you accuse Me. Accuse the god of the underworld and lastly, yourselves, because you serve him. And you also serve your gods, who abuse My name and the name of My Son. But their teaching is not My law.*

You manipulate the plants and you say it is the scientists. But I say to you that each one of you contributes his share to this, because the god of the underworld can work on this earth and in this world as he does only because you are the instruments of this god. Do you not know that everything bears information – even the "delicious" meat simmering in the pan for you animal-cannibals? Do you not know that through genetic engineering you are also manipulated, that your genes also change? Do you not know that the information in the animals that you have killed, that you consume, is information that goes into your cellular tissues and programs you accordingly? The fear, the desperation, the suffering; and the will of the god of the underworld, who now causes genetic engineering to be carried out, wants you to become ever more aggressive and that you kill each other. "Oh well," so speak your gods who serve the god of the underworld, "we are allowed to kill, just not murder." This is what your gods say. But I say to you: You shall not kill! Neither human being nor animal, nor should you defile plants and animals. And since you differentiate between killing and murdering, what is happening in your slaughterhouses? Is that killing or is it murdering? What is taking place in your wars? Is that killing or is it murdering? Dead is dead! You do not see how the souls arrive in the beyond. They themselves often do not know anymore whether they are soul, human being or animal.

Verily, verily, I say to you: One day, the hour will strike for each one of you. Happy the one who has made use of this existence on earth – not for "his own" good, but for the common good, which means: the good for all, for all, equally. On earth as it is in heaven. Everyone who creates his own good serves the god of the underworld. And everyone who wants to become rich, or is rich, is a candidate for the underworld. Do not accuse the God of the common good, the God of love and of peace, whom Jesus taught you about and thus brought to you through His life. Accuse yourselves and complain to the one whom you serve and to whom you pay homage, every day anew, through your feeling, thinking, speaking and acting!

Every seed that you deliberately mistreat is a seed of illness, so to speak, in the cells of your body. A cell is thus burdened. Recognize how much food you destroy.

Do you not know that with this you destroy yourselves? Do you not know that by doing so you are driving yourselves into hunger and ruin?

The one who gradually grows into the common good strives to be with and for his neighbor and is equal to his neighbor, on earth as it is in heaven. The one who nurtures his own good wants to be master and lord. But you lords, who think you are creation, I say to you: there is only one Lord and that is the God of Abraham, the God of Isaac, the God of Jacob, the God of all true prophets. That AM I, who speaks to you through the mouth of a prophet.

What did the people do to the prophets? They slandered, discriminated, derided, mocked and killed many of them. Do not say this was your priests, your pastors. You serve them, these gods, and thus, you are guilty with them!

What are you doing with your present prophet, called prophetess, because she is a woman? You let her be derided, mocked and discriminated against. Why? Because you do hear the words of My Son, but you seldom do them. And the one who does not do them is for the one who is against Me, for the god of the underworld!

What you are doing to your earth, this will hit you; it will be allotted to every single one of you. What you do to your neighbors, this will be allotted to both of you, or three or four of you, depending on how many you are. Weighed, measured, each will be allotted **his** part. This is why you should look at **your** part, at your guilt, and not blame your neighbor, even when he shares the blame. Jesus told you about the beam and splinter and taught you the law of remorse and forgiveness, and as Christ He has taught it to you again – a simple teaching, which raises you into heaven, but you do not want to accept it!

When you awaken in the morning you have received another day as a gift from the God of love, so that you make use of the gift, the day, by recognizing parts of your inputs, your aberrations, that is, your sins, and repent of them with the help of your Redeemer, with the Christ-spark in you, clear them up and make amends for what you can still make good. And if you no longer commit the same, the heavens will open up for you, and you will escape your world of hell.

A simple teaching. But the teaching is too simple for the crowned habitus of your gods. They are not called ones; instead they practice their profession and are paid well by their sheep, so that they live in wealth and opulence, while the poorest vegetate away and scrape together their last penny for a candle, for an "Our Father" from the god, who I Am not.

Verily, verily, I say to you: Your prayers are an abomination to Me, for you lament and complain and *do not know that you can knock and it will be opened to you, if you come with your whole heart and not with a divided one. Your songs are an abomination to Me, because you do not sound like the sound of the heavens. Your worship services are an abomination to Me, for you do not worship Me through them, but those who hold them.*

Do you not know that the Spirit of God, the love, the wisdom and the greatness that I Am dwells in you indivisibly? Only when you have learned to make use of the gift of the day, to change your ways, to repent of your sins, to clear them up and no longer commit them, will you recognize that you are My children – children of love, children of peace, children of the common good, children of the earth and not children of this world. Then you will also dispense with your negative behavior that has made of this world what it is. Then you will walk step by step in the footsteps of Jesus of Nazareth, who said to you: Follow Me, the Christ of God. Take the commandments and the Sermon on the Mount. Place them before your eyes, before your senses, and compare your misdeeds with the commandments and the Sermon on the Mount, and you will recognize each day anew whom you have served, and then you can decide whom you want to continue to serve: the God of truth, the God of unity, who I Am, the God of love – or the god of the underworld, who whispers to you again and again: Divide, bind and rule. But I say to you:

Link with your neighbor. Link with the animals, plants and minerals. And be in Me consciously. Then you will experience the God, who I AM, the God of love, a Father who created you from His whole heart and who gave you the entire heritage of the pure Being, who loves you unendingly. The pledge was Jesus; the pledge is Christ, the Redeemer-spark in every one of you. The heavens are your homeland, your eternal homeland. There, the levels of evolution are shining, the minerals; there, all the plant species are shining; there, the animals move in harmony, peace and joy, and there, the pure beings live as a unity in the stream of unity, in My law of love.

How long do you still want to continue to serve the one who dominates you? You have free will. I do not interfere in the free will of My children. I give admonishing impulses. I give help when the whole heart asks, and I give help as it is good for the soul and not as the human being wants.

*Oh recognize that My Son, your Redeemer, and I are one – **one** power, **one** entirety in each one of you. My Son, your Redeemer, is the Good Shepherd. Through the Redeemer-deed, He accepted and received you, and this, as His adoptive children, so as to lead you to Me, the primal Father, the Creator of the heavens and earth, of the pure Being. You should listen to Jesus,* *the Christ, then you will be listening to your Father, who I AM, and you will also hear the Mother, who I AM – the one stream, the one law of love. And you will receive from the heavens and you will enter the heavens, because you all come from the eternal heavens.*

Do not listen to the god of the underworld. Do not listen to the gods who flatter you. Take in hand the commandments of God and the Sermon on the Mount and examine your life. May the Ten Commandments and the Sermon on the Mount be the standard for your earthly existence. Then you will recognize the promptings of the god of the underworld and you will know what you have to do. The god of the underworld wants to fight against Me, for He wants to be the All-God, the All-power and the almighty One. But he will not achieve what he wants, for I AM the All-power and the almighty One, indivisible eternally.

Whom do you want to serve? With whom do you want to fight? And so, on whom do you declare war? On Me? Or on yourselves? On the promptings of the god of the underworld, which you have accepted and absorbed and according to which you act? Examine yourself. Each day is a gift. Make use of the day and know that deep in the very basis of your soul you are My children and remain My children, for what I beheld and created will also return to Me. But I do not force you to anything. You have freedom through the entire heritage of the Being. Do you want to keep on suffering? Do you want to vegetate away? Do you want to be tormented by illness, hunger and need? Then **you** want it this way, but not I. And then, **you** want it as the god of the underworld wants it. For he wants to enslave you; he wants to torment you; he wants you to be against each other, for he lives from this. When you are for and with one another, he receives less and less energy and has to give up. His battle is not worth it, this way or that; for when the earth bursts apart and the pure part of the earth returns, then the battle will very well continue in the purification planes, where the inputs of the human, of the sinful, are. But the stronghold will no longer exist, nor the mainstays – they are the people who serve the one who I Am not.

Verily, verily, I say to you that I AM your Father from eternity to eternity and, in the stream of the law, the entire heart as unity, Father and Mother, **one** power, **one** love, the freedom, health, joy and the well-being of each one. But you decide: Do you want to vegetate away, or do you want to live? So I say to you that I AM the life from eternity to eternity, and there is no life other than the life that I AM and that is your divine heritage. What pathways are you treading? Do you let yourselves be guided by the One Shepherd, by Christ?

Or do you let yourselves be led astray by the hirelings, who have hired you merely for their own purposes?

Through the mouth of a prophet, I have given you some insight into your world. However, when you look at this world with alert senses, with your whole heart, then you will know that the cruelties are increasing because the people let themselves be manipulated by the god of the underworld. What do you want? If you cling to this world, then you will also go under with this world. Your souls will go to corresponding places in the beyond. If you free yourselves from the doings of this world, by fulfilling My divine laws, the commandments, step by step, and thus, also the Sermon on the Mount, then you will walk in the footsteps of Jesus of Nazareth and experience the true God, who makes you free and happy through your Redeemer, Christ, the Co-Regent of the heavens.

May My earnest words reverberate in your hearts. May they enter the whole heart, only then will you be prepared to step into the footprints of Jesus of Nazareth and to follow Him, the only Shepherd. All other shepherds are mere hirelings who have hired you for their purposes.

Oh see, I AM the God who calls you through the mouth of a prophet, who calls you through Christ, My

Son, your Redeemer. I AM the God who beheld and created you and who gave you the entire heritage of the Being, so that you may live eternally in the eternal Being, in all eternity. That AM I, the God, the Father-Mother-God of love, of peace, of harmony, of unity and of the common good, the good of all. Whom do you choose: the god of your time – or the God of eternity, who I AM?

My word through the mouth of a prophet fades away. But may it reverberate in you. May the echo of the words that I have spoken through the mouth of a prophet be in every impure thought. And note well: I Am not the god of time. I AM the God of eternity.

My blessing, My love and My peace are touching you. My children, I bless the very basis of your soul. I bless your entire heart, so that your wanting may become My will.

I AM the I AM from eternity to eternity, so does it resound in infinity and also through space and time.
I AM the I AM from eternity to eternity.

The One Who Knows Me Walks at My Hand

Christ Revelation, 1991

*I Am the word of the All.
I Am in you, and you are in Me, My child.*

*Oh see: I speak to you so that you grasp Me **in you**.
For the materialistic life is drawing to an end. However, the flame of righteousness rises ever higher. I Am the love and the righteousness in God, your Father and Mine, Christ.*

Have you consciously accepted the life in your inner being? Then you live consciously in Me, and everything is manifest to you. For God, our eternal Father, has no secrets, not even from His human children. Those shrouded by secrets are you, yourselves; for you make a mystery out of what is the true life. You say: "God cannot be fathomed." Why is He unfathomable for many? Because many of My human children do not fathom themselves, they do not recognize themselves, and thus, they do not find the root of what is human in themselves.

As long as you live on the surface of your human ego, you will not find your way to the depths of the eternal Being and will not know who you are. This is why, for many, God, the eternal light, is far away. For many, God is a mystery – and yet, God, our Father, the power and the light, is near to each one.

Oh recognize that the earth gives itself to the people. Whatever man thinks, whatever he accomplishes on the earth – the earth gives itself. When a person becomes impoverished in his inner being, then he will go to that place where the earth no longer gives itself in the same measure as it does in other countries. For like attracts like: The poor soul is then also poor externally.

So do not say you are rich in your inner beings, because you receive gift after gift from the Mother Earth. Each one is called upon to ask himself: Do you receive the gifts from Mother Earth **in full awareness**? Or do you steal the gifts from Mother Earth? Can you truly say that you receive rightly from Mother Earth, because you are rich in your inner beings?

Oh see: In former lives many a one has developed an inner life. Today they repudiate it again – and nevertheless, they find themselves still on that part of the earth that gives, gives and gives. Tomorrow it may be totally different. For when a person has only taken, he becomes impoverished in his inner being. Where will the poor soul be then?

Each person must ask himself this question: Where will the poor soul be – in the spheres of purification and in the next incarnation?

See: Just as you feel, think and speak today, so will you live tomorrow. If your feelings, thoughts and words are poor, that is, if they have little life force, if they were actualized too little, then the soul will be here and there. Where? Where it is attracted to – according to its development, or its downfall.

Hear the voice of your brother and Redeemer in your inner being. It is not the words alone that bring you wisdom, but the contents of the words are filled with love, wisdom, power and care for each one of you. Verily, I want to care for you, I want to surround you, and I want to guide you to the inner life, which is the inner wealth.

Oh see, many people look only at the appearances and do not recognize what is concealed behind them. You listen to the mass media – they appear to tell the truth. If you can listen into the words, you will know how things stand with the Mother Earth, and ultimately, with the people living on the Mother Earth, with the people who act like hypocrites, who pretend something that no longer exists – namely, peace.

There is no peace any more on the earth, neither in the material layers of the earth nor in the atmosphere. The disharmonies of man have their effects in and on the earth and also in the atmosphere. Who lives in-between? Man. How? Many lead a sham existence and know they should strive for the Being. But for many there is still only the base existence: wanting to be, wanting to have, wanting to possess.

See, until now, the darkling has fulfilled this wanting for those who have input it more and more. But much is now melting away from the darkling, too. The ball is rolling, and even the dark fellow can no longer stop it. He made it start rolling, and so he will also be bowled over. Who allows himself to be impaled by this? The one who still stands in the midst of a base existence, who does not strive for the eternal Being, even though he knows the way to the eternal Being, for the Ten Commandments point the way.

Oh see and understand that you still think about yourselves way too little, namely, about your true Self, who you are. Have you become aware of this, that you are the true Self, children of the All, equipped with the powers of the All? Have you become aware of this? Then you will sin less and less, because then the sublimity of the Eternal will be active in you, and each time you take a step toward the eternal light, you will become clearer, your consciousness brighter – and then you will very gradually look into the life, God, and grasp in your inner being that God has no secrets. God gives Himself.

Are the fruits in front of your secrets? The person says: "No, because I see them." As long as you see them with your physical eyes, even the fruits are a secret to you. Because you have not yet grasped in your inner being that each fruit speaks to you and is thus in communication with you.

Have you attained the inner greatness? Do you sense God's majesty in you? Then you can see how close God is to you – yes, He looks at you through the fruits. He looks at you through the eyes of the animals, through the blooming flowers, through grasses, bushes and trees. He looks at you through every mineral, through the simplest stone, through the speck of dust and the grain of sand.
 If you have fathomed the depths of life, then you have found your way back to the very basis, to the true life – and you are rich in your inner being. You do not need to worry about tomorrow – it **is** taken care of.
 Even when the materialistic world collapses – I know how to lead those who live close to the very basis or are already living in the very basis. I, Christ, know the pathways and footbridges. I can guide you over roaring rivers, over the earth that is breaking apart, over hot stones, over seething mountains.
 I know you. And the one who knows Me walks at My hand. Who knows Me? Only the one who knows himself. Do you know yourself? If so, then there are no

secrets for you. The very basis, in which you then live, has no secrets. For God, the Father of us all, has given infinity as a whole to each one of us.

You are infinity. I Am infinity.
You are the All and I Am the All.
If you speak the language of the All, then you understand Me, because you know yourself. Then you also know Me.

What is summer? Summer is light. Do you have the inner light? Then you know Me. If you have the inner light, then you know each fruit, each animal, each blade of grass, each stone. No plant is foreign to you. You know the path of the stars and planets, because you know the law of life, you, who are the law itself.

O My brother, My sister, do not say: "The path to the eternal Being is still so far." See, the path is so near. It is here. Do you know where? In every feeling, in every thought, in every word and in every action is the path, the Being – Am I.

Turn back! Transform the base energy into positive power – and you will no longer say: "The path is so far."

Now, at this moment, a selfless thought – and you sense and feel Me, the Being.

Now, at this moment, the fruit of life recognized – and you know the path; you know Me, for I Am everything in all things.

*If you know yourself, then you know Me.
If you know the fruits, then you know Me.*

Be ready to accept the life, for the materialistic life is dwindling. God draws closer to the one who loves selflessly. The gifts of love are being offered to you – do you love them? Ask yourself! Do you love the gifts of life? Do you love the fruits that you see with your physical eyes – not only to still your hunger, but because they are a part of you? Only then will you begin to love God, your Father.

Brother, sister, see: It is already past 12 o'clock on the great earth globe. Where do you stand in your life? Do you not yet thirst for the love of the Father? Then it could be that in some place or other you will be dying of thirst and hungering for righteousness.
For just as the causes break over the people more and more, so do I radiate into this world and into the spheres of purification. I radiate the Inner Path to you. I radiate your life to you, the life of us all, the law of selfless love. Happy the one who recognizes why God, our eternal Father, pours out the horn of plenty over mankind – because shortly the materialistic world will come to an end more and more, and here and there it will be over and done with.
Until all this has happened, many of you will still experience much – the one, suffering, the other, joy,

just as he has inflicted it upon himself. But in Me, Christ, is the turning back. In Me, Christ, is the turning within; for I dwell in you – the path goes inward. For I, Christ, Am in you. Where do you seek Me? I Am in you. Wherever you are – I Am in you.

Remember this as this materialistic world is thrown out of joint more and more, as prosperity trembles and shakes – and the person only then realizes his condition. There will be no more talk of prosperity then. Oh think about this wisely! My words are admonishing. But even as admonishing as they are – they radiate care. I want to care for you; I want to lavish care and attention on you; I want to lead you to the promised land, to safe ground, to the inner light.

Come! I am calling you. Come – I, Christ, take My sheep to pasture. Come – I lead you to the safe meadows of life and make lambs of you. Come, you sheep! I, Christ, Am here – in you, My brother, in you, My sister. Have you recognized Me? Then you have also recognized yourself, and you will fathom the depths of life, the very basis of the Being – yourself.

Come, and be. Awaken, so that there will be peace in you; for only through peaceful people will peace come to the purifying earth. I Am with you, in you, in the fruit – everywhere I Am the life. I Am the peace and *the Prince of Peace for the inner kingdom that will come to the purified earth. It is building up little by little. Are you part of it? Then you are **with** Me.*

I Am peace.
I radiate My peace to you, so that there will be peace in you.

Peace.

Are You Servile to the God of the Underworld and His Idols?

God-Father Revelation, 1997

I Am who I AM, the nameless One.

People in the various nations of this earth have various names for Me, the I AM. One calls Me God, another Jehovah, still others, the Primordial Principle or the eternal Self, or the Eternal or the Being. Still other names are given to Me, the I AM, but I Am the nameless One, the eternally streaming flow. I AM in you, O man, the I AM. I Am in every stone the I AM. In every star, in every power, in every atom Am I the I AM. I Am the I AM in each plant, in each animal. I, the I AM, Am everything, and that which I Am, the totality, is also in the material form.

O man, you are the carrier of the I AM. Are you aware of this? Wherever you look, in everything is the I AM, the nameless One. It is the eternal law; it is the streaming Spirit.

Many call me God, but God is in you, O man, the I AM, and according to your divine nature, you are an image of the I AM and are divine. Many people worship Me as the Father. Oh recognize: Out of the impersonal, the streaming flow, the Spirit, which I AM, I gave Myself form, just as I gave all pure beings the form out of the I AM, the stream. I Am the Father, the form, out of the I AM. If your inner eyes are opened, if you are divine again, then you see yourself as the pure being, as the image of your Father, whom you behold, as Being; for out of the I AM, the omnipresent power, I gave Myself form, so that My children, My sons and My daughters, could behold Me, face to face. However, if your countenance, O man, is veiled, then your eyes see only what you have created yourself: sin. If your eyes have become pure, then you perceive in your heart the I AM, the eternally streaming flow – it is **the life**. The life is the I AM. Can you see it? You experience the life in your movements, in your manner, but the life will continue to be effective in you until you have become the life yourself, that is, a being that has taken on form out of Me, the spirit being.

O you people in all the nations of this earth, many of you call Me Father and worship Me, the Father, in the Lord's Prayer. But do you prove yourselves as children of the eternal Father? Or have many of you become hell-like in your worship of the god of the underworld?

Look into your world, and you see the chaos, the chaos of every individual who has turned away from Me. It is the world karma. Everyone has a share in this world karma. Many a one says: "But where is my guilt?" Examine and monitor your thoughts and you will recognize a partial guilt.

Why do I speak through the mouth of a prophet? Because you cannot understand Me, your Father, anymore! You no longer hear Me in your hearts, because your hearts become ever colder, totally according to the will of the god of the underworld. And so, you are his subjects and feel glad and happy, so to speak, when you have a small property that you call your own. What is your own then? Your own is the heavens, and as long as you do not open this up, you are servile to the god of the underworld and his gods.

You have allowed intermediaries to slide between Me and you. In general, I call them your theologians. You call your theologians your so-called church leaders. You bestow honors upon them and call them worthy ones, but in the Lord's Prayer you pray: Father. You address Me as your Father and God, but you award dignities to the sinners by calling them worthy ones.

I ask you, My children: What do you carry in your head? A cavity – or a brain that is meant for thinking and weighing? But as long as your intermediaries manipulate you, you will think the way they want you to. And your intermediaries want you to attune yourself to them and not to God, your Father, who I Am. As long as a person does not weigh things, he remains a sinner and pays homage to sin and the sinners, because he looks to the sinners who call themselves worthy ones.

Oh see, in this way, many have turned away from Me. They fear the God of love, who I Am, and think the intermediaries can help them, by rendering God favorable to the sinners. Oh, you children, you have become foolish ones!

Eliminate your "intermediaries" and know and feel that I Am the I AM in you, the great love.
Know that I love you.
Know that I help you.
Know that I guide you back to Me through My Son, your Redeemer.
Know that I Am the life and you are eternal life.
Go into your inner being. Pray to Me in your heart, in the very basis of your soul, and fulfill your prayers, step by step. And if you want to get to know Me still better, then look at the Ten Commandments, which I gave mankind through Moses. Feel into the Sermon on the Mount of Jesus. Then you will know what you have to do, in order to grow closer to Me, God, your Father.

O human child, you draw closer to Me solely in your heart, in yourself, and never through intermediaries!

Oh recognize that you have lost the inner perception. You have lost the ability to feel. You no longer know the meaning of community and the common good, the good of all. Many are focused solely on themselves and have shut themselves off from their feelings, their subtle sensations. Thus, many have become marionettes who, without thinking, serve the god of the underworld and his gods.

And many a one asks: "When I sin, then You punish me, O God!" O child, in My entire law of love there is no punishment. You believe in the astral law "What a person sows, he will reap." This is the punishment – it is you who punish yourself through your sowing, through your sin.

Oh recognize that as long as a person is focused solely on himself, he has no way of relating to his neighbor and certainly not to the animal, plant and mineral worlds, nor to the stars and planets. He feels that he is the so-called "super God," and yet, he is merely a slave to the god of the underworld and his gods.

Oh recognize and grasp that this, your world, cannot exist in the long run. Generally speaking, this world has already fallen into the abyss. But the god of the underworld still wants to save what can be saved. With his gods, he has withdrawn to his base, the world, in order to preserve what can still be preserved through manipulation, so as to continue to fight against Me *from his base, the world. You, every single one of you, must gradually come to realize that the whole atmosphere is pouring down on this world, including the atmospheric chronicle in which the whole history of mankind is stored, all that is not yet atoned for. Your illnesses, your hardships, your worries, your epidemics and much more come from you, yourselves. It is **you**, who have entered this filth, and now it is coming back to you.*

You people in all the nations of this earth, have you not yet recognized that you are being manipulated, that you are supposed to be brought into line? Have you not yet noticed that the middle sector of a nation is supposed to be dissolved? Spoken with your words, it is the middle class. You are all supposed to become slaves, conscious subjects of the god of the underworld. The god of the underworld and his gods try using all possible means to preserve everything and to create an artificial atmospheric chronicle, so to speak, via your so-called technology. All this is happening in your world more and more, because the atmosphere is pouring down upon you and all the filth that you have entered into the atmosphere. The god of the underworld tells himself: "I can preserve many a thing through genetic engineering." And he will also not shy away from people, from your bodies, because he needs you as willing slaves, as laborers, as those brought into line, who have only one thought, and it is: "Me, everything for me, only for me! My neighbor doesn't matter – battle, war, destruction, murder, manslaughter, rape" and much more.

Oh recognize that when he preserves you, too – for he has already preserved many a one – the hour will come when the external shell will dissolve and the soul withdraws from the shell; yes, it must withdraw, for the I AM is in the soul, and it is immortal. It cannot be destroyed or manipulated. I Am the breath in you, O man. When the breath leaves your body, the soul continues to breathe. Here, the god of the underworld can try whatever he wants – I have created the pure in you and it returns to Me, even if it is over many cycles in the spheres of purification, where it is said to be: expiation.

And many a one asks himself: "What will I expiate?" O My child, sense and feel along with Me. I will give you some pictures, and if you are honest, you will experience aspects of what can come to you in the soul realms, but also in this or a future incarnation.

What is your attitude toward your neighbor?
Is your neighbor a part of your life?
Or are you indifferent toward him?
You are wealthy and prestigious. Oh see, does all this belong to you? If you have not learned to share, in order to gradually enter the good for all, the common

good, then you will become poor in another incarnation, or you will experience in the spheres of purification what you have not let your neighbor have.

I give you more pictures. You are sitting at your meal, eating meat and sausage. These are portions of your second neighbors, the animals. Do you know how this animal, parts of which you are eating, had to live in barns? Do you know how it was slaughtered? Do you know at all that when the blood is still flowing, even if the heart has stopped beating, people and animals can sense, they can still feel? This and much more is in the piece of meat that you are consuming; it is the information that passes into your physical life and, in time, will also manipulate your genes.

All of you accept the so-called organ transplantation. Do you not know that when a person dies and the blood is still flowing, that this person can still sense and feel? But you tear the organs out of his body for the next person. What kind of people have you become? And then you pray to me and say that I would punish you!

You clear-cut the forests. You cut down bushes and trees that are filled with sap. When the sap is flowing, the tree and the bush also feel. The minerals are brutally taken from the ground, the stones ground up – do you not know that the I AM is in everything and that every form of life feels, even the smallest stone that you tread on? It gives itself up for the light-filled beings, but it must also give itself up for the brutality that frequently calls itself man.

Many of you say that animals have infectious diseases. Who infected them – God or man? You take in this information and experience the infectious disease in your physical body. Who is to blame? God? Or yourselves?

See all of this in your pictures! The animal in your slaughterhouses, hung up, that is, hanged – it bleeds and feels. Animals in the most confined spaces. They are suffering. Feel! Animals in your so-called transports. Feel how many an animal dies in the most terrible way. Feel into your laboratories. Animal experiments. Here an injection, there an injection, kept and observed in the tightest spaces.

If all of this happened to you, what would you say then? You will experience all of these pictures, and according to your part in it, you will experience the pain, the torment of the animals, the plants and the minerals.

When the blows of fate hit you on this side of life, then you accuse Me. Complain to the god of the underworld and his gods, whom you have served and serve in a ruthless manner toward life. And you are just as ruthless toward your own physical body, but also toward your soul, which, at the latest, will languish in *the spheres of purification, for in proportion to its participation, it will have to experience what the person tolerated in this world. What good does your silence do? What good does your protesting do? It is all you can do. It will not help you. The god of the underworld strides onward, until a pole comes into movement and then it is over with this world. Note well: with this world, not with this earth. Where will it go on? In the spheres of purification. There, the disembodied souls will find themselves again, in the same condition. And so, you take your condition to the spheres of purification. There, it it is about expiation. There, your eyes are directed toward your inputs, toward your pictures. They are similar to those that I have briefly described to you.*

Many people are merciless and pitiless. They remain merciless and pitiless and call for Me in the last hour of their physical existence. Oh see, the commandments given through Moses were not given to you for the last hour, nor was the Sermon on the Mount of Jesus! These divine laws for a higher life were given to you for your earthly existence, so that you may recognize your sins, and with the help of the Redeemer-Spirit in you, the Christ of God, repent of the sins you have recognized, clear them up and no longer commit them. This is what it takes to grow into the inner life. For this, no intermediaries are needed. What is necessary is a light-filled mind that still knows how to weigh what is good and what is disgraceful.

Oh see, you, yourselves, every single one of you, has the freedom to torment yourself or to liberate yourself from these sins with the help of the redeeming power in you. Every day is a gift from the heavens, a gift of the I AM, who I Am, so that you will take the steps toward Me. For this, it is not an intermediary that is needed, but good will, in order to find your way out of slavery to a God-conscious person, who knows what it means to fulfill the laws of love and peace. And if you do not do this, you will degenerate more and more. This is what the god of the underworld and his gods want.

What good does it do you if you protest today and tomorrow eat the flesh of your second neighbors, the animals, once more? What good does it do you if you see much that is inconsistent, that is not divine – and remain silent? The one who remains silent is saying that he does the same and similar things. What means do you already have in hand to proceed against the god of the underworld, who holds you prisoner? It is solely the I AM, and this is in you. It is your true being. It is your true life. It is the eternal law of love, of peace, of freedom and unity. Do you want to attain these inner, highest values? Then measure your feeling, sensing, thinking, speaking and acting against the commandments that I gave through Moses, and against the Sermon on the Mount of Jesus. With the help of your Redeemer, Christ, in you, repent of what is against this; clear it up with your neighbor, but also with your second neighbor through Me, the Creator-Spirit. Clear it up with all of nature, and do such things no more. This is the path out of slavery. Then you will gradually begin to think in a divine way.

But do not forget: Then, the god of the underworld and his gods will attack you, because the one who becomes an inner thinker becomes dangerous. This is why the middle sector of the people is to be eliminated, because the middle sector strives toward its gods, and too many gods are too harmful for the god of the underworld. They come into disunity and fight against each other, just as the demons also fight against each other in the regions of the astral worlds.

Oh recognize in your hearts and grasp with your senses that you have no need for intermediaries; instead, you need the spiritual principles of life, which are your divine heritage. Fulfill these more each day, and you will become God-conscious thinkers. And the more people there are who do this, the more quickly a great, mighty, God-conscious unity of people will develop, people who call themselves brothers and sisters, who very gradually come together to establish the Kingdom of God that has been proclaimed on this earth, the kingdom of love and peace. But this will not come flying down from heaven – it can come solely through you, through every single one of you, for in the very basis of your souls you are children of heaven. With your hellish thoughts, you have turned yourselves into slaves. Stop! Turn back, and know that I Am the I AM, and I Am very near to you, My child, to every one of you. Where? **In** your thought. **In** your word. **In** your sensation and **in** your feeling. I knock on your feeling. Listen – it is your conscience. I knock in your heart. I rap and knock in your word. Listen, and examine your words, to see whether they are God-pleasing. Examine your thoughts.

You say, that to draw closer to God, to Me, would be very difficult. O, you foolish children! How far you have removed yourselves from God, your Father, who I Am! A touch of honesty, a touch of good will, of turning back, of turning toward the inner life, which I Am – and you will feel the help of your Redeemer, and you will perceive the tender breath of God in your breath, for you become calmer and your breath deeper. However, the prerequisite is that you **want** to escape from the slavery of sin.

Take in hand the commandments that I gave through Moses. Take in hand the Sermon on the Mount of Jesus. Become absorbed in the meaning of the divine laws. Do not merely read the word. Contemplate the word as *a whole and ask for enlightenment – and it will be given to you. Oh see, this is the simplest, but also the direct, path with Christ, your Redeemer, to Me, your eternal Father.*

Is this too simple for you? You think that I Am as complicated as your intermediaries who created an illusory structure around the great God, who I Am. However, all of this illusory structure is merely the ego, the base ego of the intermediaries. They want to keep you in this illusory structure, as if to preserve you, so that you look solely to the intermediaries, instead of to God, your Father.

*Oh see, as long as you look with the eyes of sin, you will see only your sins, in turn. Learn. Learn, to feel into your neighbor, whom you disparage, whom you hate, whom you envy, and you will experience the fine breath of God, who I Am. Then you will have the strength to make peace with your neighbor. If your neighbor does not want this, then **you** keep the peace in your thoughts, words and actions, but also in your feelings and sensations. This is the way.*

Feel into the animal. It feels according to its level of consciousness. Feel into it. It senses, because life is the finest sensation. Can you then mistreat it? Can you then beat it? Can you then consume it? Feel into the life of the trees, of the bushes, the flowers. Yes, feel into every stone. Practice, and you will experience the breath of the I AM. Can you cut down the trees that are filled with sap, taking their life, as it were?

Oh see, from these subtlest sensations, which you will then attain, you will gradually feel what it means to live in Me. You will then strive toward the higher ideals and values step by step. And in time, you will learn to share with those who also share. From this, the result is the common good and the good for all. This is the unity in the law of life, and this is, in turn, your divine heritage.

But each one has his free will, to torment himself, to mistreat himself, to write himself off as a slave to this god of the underworld – or to enter into his divine heritage. The I AM, the Spirit, the life, does not pressure you. But the god of the underworld pressures you to do this and that. At the moment you feel the pressure, you are supposed to serve **him**. But I do not pressure you to do anything. I exert no pressure. I gave you My Son, your heavenly brother. The Redeemer-power flowed from Him, for every soul and for every person. He sacrificed Himself for mankind. His Spirit remained in Me and is in Me. It is **one** Spirit, **one** love, which is effective in you. Ask yourselves the question: Whom do you want to serve? The god of the underworld – or gradually, very gradually, the heavenly, eternal laws, the I AM? If you have learned to serve the divine, then you are consciously sons and daughters of God again, *steadfast in My Spirit, steadfast in your divine heritage, which I Am. It is only in this way that you can make Mother Earth – not this world anymore, but Mother Earth – into a blooming oasis, that you can help her become a blooming oasis, give heart to the life, so to speak, so that Mother Earth may become ever more light-filled, ever sunnier, and a life can develop, of which you now, as human beings, still have no inkling. For the seeds of the earth bear the life in themselves, the I AM. It is another nature. It is other animals. This will emerge through other people, who live God-consciously, who prove themselves to be sons and daughters of God.*

Examine your earthly existence, which consists of your feeling, sensing, thinking, speaking and acting. And ask yourselves: What do you want? This decision lies not only in your hands; it is also written in your mind. And the one who still knows how to weigh things, will now know what he has to do.

I Am the I AM.

Realize, My child, I Am in you. I Am very close to you. I Am your true life. I Am the love, the kindness, the gentleness, and for every willing one, the grace, which begins when you want this, that is, when you turn back and fulfill step by step the spiritual principles of life, which are found in the Ten Commandments and in the Sermon on the Mount.

You people in all the nations of this earth, realize that I Am the I AM, the life. Whatever you call Me – the one who addresses Me with his heart, with a request that comes from the very basis of his soul, will receive My answer, no matter what he calls Me, primordial source or primordial principle, God or God-Father, Jehovah or Being, it does not matter. I know you, O human child! Your true being is in communication with Me. If you draw from this source and ask with all your heart, then it will be given to you. Grace and mercy will be granted to you.

So receive the words very consciously. Take them in. They are strength and blessing.
I Am the I AM eternally.
I Am the I AM eternally.

I Make All Things New

God-Father Revelation, 1991

I Am the I Am, the word of infinity.

I Am the I Am, the power in all stars and planets, the light in all souls and men.

I Am the Creator-power in every animal, in every plant, in every stone.

I Am the All and the law of the All.

The one who speaks My voice has become the law of the All; he is conscious life in Me.

I Am the omnipresence, the stream, the Being. From the stream of life, I took on form, that is, I took shape. I became a spirit being, your Father, whom you also call the Father-Mother-God. From the stream of the All which I, the Being, Am, I myself took on form, yes, shape. And so, I Am the All that has become form, your Father.

May the one who can grasp it, grasp it. May the one who wants to leave it, leave it. But recognize that just as I became form, I have formed you. You, too, came forth from the stream of the All; you took on spiritual form. This form is called the spirit being, the life-principle of the heavens. As a result of this, in spirit, you are My images and My children. Now, you are human beings and speak the language of man. This is why I took an instrument for Myself, a human being, in order to speak through My instrument in your language, with your words, so that you, who are human beings, can understand Me.

But recognize that My holy word is the All and the law. It is contained in each physical word. May the one who truly wants to hear Me grasp the meaning of the words; for in the physical word I Am the word, the law of infinity.

My children, I call you – also in the name of My Son, your Redeemer – to become aware of the filiation of God, to become aware that you are My children. I Am immortal and you are immortal. Even though the shell, the person, fades, withers and dies, know that in the shell is the soul, which will become a spirit being again through Christ, an inhabitant of the heavens; for in reality, deep in your shells, you are children of the heavens. Your path goes from the earth via the stars and planets to Me, to the eternal Being.

Recognize and grasp and feel My word in your hearts; for I speak My word into your hearts, so that you may grasp the meaning.

Oh recognize that through the Fall-thought many of My children went away from Me. For they thought *that they could dissolve the eternal forms of the Being again, so that it would again be as it was before creation, streaming spirit in infinity, without spiritual forms. But I Am the eternal perfect principle. What I created and create is immutable. It cannot be dissolved. That was a delusion of the particle manifest out of Me.*

Listen, My children in the earthly garment: Many of My children went forth, and I gave them a quantum of spiritual power to take with them, so that outside the eternal Being they could create their suns and their worlds. Verily, I say to you: I gave them this quantum because I loved them and love them. This quantum contained parts of spiritual suns and planets. This quantum contained animals, plants and minerals. All these forms of life belong to the eternal Being and thus, they belong to My children – whether they move in the pure Being or whether they draw away from Me, in order to arrange their life as they conceived it and still conceive it today.

The world of conceptions of My children has become large. This is why many no longer believe in Me, the speaking God. They let theologians speak and so-called Bible experts. They let the rulers of all nations speak and let themselves be misled by all their talking. Many people no longer realize that I Am the speaking God in them. For them, it is their gods who speak: their wishful dreams, their egocentricities, their vehicles, their arro-

gance, their greed and their claims to power. These are the gods of this world. They led and lead many, very many, astray.

Through this constant misdirection, very gradually, the material cosmos emerged; this planet earth developed and very gradually, the shells that you call human beings, as well. As a result, you are human beings, that is, shells, in which the eternal life dwells, I, the inner light, in each one of you.

Only the fewest of My children recognize the spiritual principles of inner life and even less their own law, which says: What you sow, you will reap. Everyone thinks that the other one will have to reap it, and not himself. These obsessions have led people to without, into the world of the senses and sensual desires. As a result, the speaking God can no longer be perceived, for I Am the word of the heart. But the one who no longer has a heart for his neighbor, for the animals and plants, is heartless and is not in communication with Me, but with the powers that affect the whole material system in a destructive way.

My children, the quantum of spiritual power in the material stars and planets, the quantum of spiritual power in the animals, the plants and human beings is largely used up, that is, reversed into negative energy. This means that neither stars nor human beings can live in the long run, because I Am the spirit power, the life. Consequently, diseases, miseries, disasters, wars, starvation and pestilence will increase, for very gradually a new heaven and a new earth is emerging.

Apart from this, the cup is full. What flows over the edge, will cause even more disasters on the earth, even more illness and suffering than in times past.

Recognize and grasp in your hearts, My children: The cup is full – here and there it is running over. In this way, parts of nations, yes, entire nations will be taken away. The earth is cleansing itself from the trivia of this world. The circus of the human ego is dissolving and all the actors and make-up artists who do not turn back will fall into the floods. The cup is full. The quantum of divine energy is used up, transformed into negative energy. Over the course of time, man cannot live with only negative energy; for the negative energy is the energy of cause and effect, and what man has sown is coming back to him.

Recognize how the way to the causes proceeds. The person thinks, thinks, feels, feels, speaks, speaks, and acts – all of it negative. By doing so, he transforms the positive power into negative energies. No energy is lost. Every thought wants to find itself again. And where will it find itself, and where has it found itself? First, in your consciousness. The more often you think, feel, *speak and do the same and like things, the greater become the programs in your consciousness, in your brain. In time, this energy goes into the subconscious and, at the same time, into the consciousness and subconscious of the cells of your body. As you continue to feel, think, speak and act in a like way, the negative energies enter your soul, which is the book of life.*

This process that takes place in you, at the same time takes place in the material stars and the purification planes. As a result, every cell in your physical body is registered in the material stars. Every burden is registered in the purification planes. All Being remains in the Being, in the Eternal.

It is in this way that the causes are built up.

Heaven, infinity, is constant movement. The stars in the purification planes are touched by predetermined cycles. The stars of the purification planes radiate through the material stars. The material stars affect the souls of the human beings. Via the person's soul, it enters his brain and from his brain, his cells. There, in the cellular tissues, the cause then breaks out.

But before all this happens, the energy of the day makes itself known, the guardian spirit makes itself known; for a being of light has been assigned to each one of you. The one who does not live consciously does not hear the impulses of the day; he does not hear the admonishing impulses of his guardian spirit. He con-

tinues to live in his negative world of thoughts, in hatred, in strife, in quarrel, in envy, in resentment, in sensuality and much more.

In this way, the causes were built up and continue to build up, and via the stars, they, in turn, bear fruit – as effects.

My children, the cup is now full; this means that people's bodies will disintegrate more and more, if the person does not transform the negative energy into positive energy in time, through the power of the Redeemer-Spirit that is in every soul, in every person.

At the same time, more and more parts of the material stars disintegrate. In time, whole stars, whole sun systems, parts of galaxies, – that is, milky ways – will disintegrate, because the bodies of people are disintegrating. Yes, death is gaining ground, for now the time has come in which I make all things new.

A new heaven and a new earth are emerging, because a higher human race will develop. The age of the Spirit brings people of the Spirit, people with a higher consciousness, who are in communication with the eternal Being, with the eternal law, which I Am. They will truly possess the earth, the purified earth. And so, what was revealed long ago will take place: a new heaven. The material stars are changing. Matter will appear again, but in a higher form, with higher degrees of consciousness, just as this earth will be matter again, but of a finer substance, because the shells, the people, will also be of a finer substance, since souls filled with more light will live in the shells.

My children, I call you and call you also in the name of My Son, your Redeemer: Turn back!

To turn back means to reflect upon your spiritual origin and to clear up what is human in you with Christ. Clear up your past, otherwise you will keep turning in the same circle of your negative feelings, thoughts, words and actions. Clear up your past, so that you can live more and more consciously in the day; for the day points out what wants to show up in the body: suffering, illness, distress and much more. The day gives impulses before the effect breaks out on your physical body. Your guardian spirit gives you impulses; your conscience tells you many a thing. Be alert!

This is what it means to turn back. And if you turn back, taking the path of true remorse, of asking for forgiveness, of forgiving, of making amends and, if you do not commit your faults again, then you will transform the negative energy, which is in your cells, in your soul, into positive energy, into spirit energy, into My power, into the law of love. At the same time, it changes in the material stars. At the same time, it changes in the purification planes. In this way, you *very gradually make contact again with Me, the inner light. Thus, you go within. You purify your base senses, because you reduce your passions, your negative thoughts, feelings, words and actions.*

You ennoble yourself in this way. You journey inward more and more, to the indwelling light, which I Am. You can thus transform many a wrongdoing that wants to break in over you as an effect.

Everything that you have caused is thus recorded in your brain; it is recorded in your cellular tissues; it is written in your soul, registered in the material stars and also in the purification planes, where your souls will be after the shell passes away.

If the bodies disintegrate, then the stars disintegrate. But this energy is not lost – it transforms itself into a higher form. In this way, the Fall will dissolve very gradually. My children return to Me, to Me, their Father, for I keep all of you in My heart. And you will return to Me in My heart, in the mighty All-stream, and will consciously be My images once more, pure beings – just as I have beheld and created you and as I bear you in My heart.

Children, My Son, your Redeemer, and I, your Father, want to lead you back; we want to spare you disgrace, illness, need, infirmity, suffering and death.

But each one has free will. The one who does not want to listen will feel. Through your free will, you have also created your ego-law. It is the causal law for every individual, the law that says: What you sow is what you will reap. It is not your neighbor who reaps it – **you** reap it according to the principle: Like draws to like. Your seed is, in turn, your harvest. Where? In and on your physical body, and later, as soul in the spheres of purification; for all negative energy, that is, the unlawful energy, has to be transformed into spirit power. Each one brings with him what he has taken as spirit power and transformed. He transforms it back into spiritual energy again, so that the quantum of spiritual energy will be brought back into the All-stream, into the law of love, which I Am, out of which you are and in which you will live eternally.

My children, My word sounds in many material ears. Many questions come up from this. Fear and worry emerge. If you want to take My word apart with your human ego, with your sensory world, you will gain nothing. But if you move My word in your hearts, then you will grasp the meaning of the earthly word, that is, the content of the physical word – and you will experience in your hearts what I have placed into the word of man. This is My law, My word. The one who can grasp it, grasps much more. He realizes that this materialistic world is not only standing at the edge of the abyss, but parts of it have already slipped into the depths.

No matter what your theologians, your governing ones say: Many of them are controlled. For the world can pretend something only to the world – but not to those who are from the Spirit, that is, those who shine a light more penetratingly on the statements of the theologians, of the rulers and also of the scientists. The one who can do this hears what they want to conceal in what they say.

Where is the rescue, My children? Where is the anchor that you can hold on to? Is it your neighbor? Is it money and possessions; is it wealth, power and prestige? All of this will pass away, but My love for My children will remain – eternally.
I Am the speaking God. My children, I do not forsake you; for I Am the omnipresent power, the inner light in you, in you – in each one of you. I Am the inner light in your second neighbors, the animals, the plants, the minerals. I Am the light in the stars. No matter where you look – I Am present everywhere. And if you, My child, have learned to behold, if you have learned to perceive, this means that you then perceive Me in you; for all forms of life are in each one of you as essence and power. The light in the small animal is not outside of you. The light in the plants, in the suns, in the stars is not outside of you – it is in you. Countless forces of the All are active in you – I have made your spiritual body with them. As a result, you can perceive Me in

everything only in you – and the perception takes place when you go within, when you cleanse yourself, when, with Christ, your Redeemer, you transform into positive energy the negativity that you have inflicted upon yourself. Then you will experience how rich you are, My child.

Verily, you are rich! You are, as I, your Father, Am, the All that has taken on form. You are My image. Be aware of this! See, I want you to become the word of the All again, yes, that you be the word of the All again. And so, become the word of the All gradually, until you are totally and completely the All again. Then you, too, will speak the word of the All, the law of love.

Oh see, then you will no longer need to ask – you will know it, because you are wise. You will no longer need to look here and there – you will experience it in you, because you are in Me.

Child, recognize that you bear infinity in you as essence and power. Turn back, and become what you are in My heart: the pure being, eternally.

My child, you are on a journey – when will you end the journey? You determine this. Whatever you meet on your journey, joy and sorrow – you determine this. And so, when you reach your goal is determined by you. Whether you go to another incarnation – you determine this. Your seed tells you this, and you experience your seed daily, hourly and by the minute. Clear up what you experience! Then you will experience and overcome ever more of your seeds; for Christ, your Redeemer, helps you to gain self-recognition and also helps you to achieve transformation, by granting you the strength to transform the negative.

My child, what do you want to do? If you do not want to accept My word, then look into the world. The materialistic world is dying from the bottom up. Where will you stay? When will it hit you? How will it hit you? You determine this.
See, My Son, your Redeemer, and I, your Father, reach out our hand to you. You have the way to the heart of love, to the light in you, which I Am. You have the day, the hour, every moment. Make use of the day – and you will experience yourself. You have a companion at your side, a being that is invisible to you. It places impulses into your conscience. You are helped in manifold ways and means, My child. The heavens are open, and the beings of light go to the people and to the souls in the spheres of purification.

My Spirit is active in every person, in every soul. But, My child, you determine whether you want to accept the help or not. And so, you determine your path. Where does it lead you? If you want to know, then ask yourself. To where you think, what you feel, what you speak and do, this is your identification. At the same time, it points out your path, not that of your neighbor – your path, My child.

My child, know that the speaking God, who I Am, who reveals Himself through a human mouth, also wants to speak in you very consciously. Therefore, go inward, yes, heavenward, for heaven is in you – just as hell can also be in you, if you build on your burdens more and more and thus vegetate away in your burdens, until your body is marked. What then? Suffering and infirmity. Why? Ask yourself. You can give the answer yourself.

My child, a new heaven and a new earth are emerging. The era of the Spirit is approaching with might and with it a new human race, a new culture in the light of the truth.

I make all things new. I Am the transforming power in every person, in every soul, in the animals, plants and stones. I Am the transforming power in the stars. I Am. I make all things new. If you want to become new, then go within, into your inner being, and realize that you are the temple of the Holy Spirit, that I dwell in you: I, the inner light; I, the light of the All; I, the stream of the All; I, the Being in all things; I, your Father, from eternity to eternity.

Child, look into the word eternity. This word, too, is your own, because as a being you live in Me eternally

– from eternity to eternity. Ask yourself if you truly want this. If yes, My child, then you sense Me at this moment; for My word is radiation and touches you in your heart. Hope, confidence, faith and an inkling of what it means to love selflessly draw into you.

Child, truly, I Am your Father. And if you live in Me, then you speak My word, and the instrument is no longer needed, and then I no longer talk to you through the mouth of a human being. Then, you are the word again; you have become the law and you speak the law of life. Then you no longer ask – you are.

Child, feel in your heart that I love you. I love you, My child. This is why I sent My Son to this earth. He walked over it as Jesus of Nazareth. My child, I love you; this is why we, My Son and I, reveal ourselves again through the mouth of a human being.

My child, take the radiation of love with you into your further earthly existence. I radiate My Father-love to you, into your heart.

My child, I love you! I do not want you to suffer. I do not want you to be sick. I do not want you to be hungry. I do not want you to be without shelter. I do not want you to live in regions of disaster. Child, I want to rescue you – but you determine this. For you have the free will to turn back, or to continue to live in sin, in your sin.

Child, My child, I love you. My child, I love you. Hear Me in your heart! My child, I, your Father, embrace you. Feel the secureness in Me. Take refuge in your inner being – I Am there. Child, My child, I love you! Come back to the Father-heart. You live in Me eternally, from eternity to eternity.

My child, if you no longer hear Me through the mouth of a human being – child, I speak to you through the rays of the sun, through the suns, through the stars, through the entire All. I speak to you through all the forms of life. I speak in you. Go within; purify your soul – and you will become My word again. My child, I love you.
My love is My blessing for you. It flows into the spheres of purification. It flows to all people. It flows to the animals, plants, stones and minerals. It flows – it is the love.

My child, through the mouth of a human being, I become silent in word, but I remain the speaking God – in your heart, everywhere, in the wind, in the storm; everywhere, in the rain, in every drop of water, Am I. Child, you are surrounded by My power. Accept it, become – and be!

I Am the Eternal One, eternally. You are in Me, eternally, in all eternity.

When the Hour Strikes ...

Christ Revelation, 1998

I Am the truth. The light of the heavens is the light of revelation, the light of the Christ of God, who I Am.
My peace and My love I bring to you.

Oh see, the one who strives for the truth opens his heart for the truth, and the truth, which I Am, does not keep you waiting: It serves; it helps; it resolves and redeems. But the one who does not open his heart for the truth cannot receive from the truth, which I Am.

Oh see, the light of revelation radiates to all people; the light of revelation, which I Am, radiates to all souls in the spheres of purification, for I Am the way, the truth and the life. As Jesus of Nazareth, I taught the path to the Father and, as a human being, I lived it as an example. As the Christ of God, I again revealed and reveal to you the path to the Father, but you know that I can only offer it to you – each one of you must walk it himself, today, tomorrow, in the coming times or generations. And so, it depends on you, because you have free will.
So many a one says: "I am on the path to God, my Father." But when he is asked: Do you keep peace with

your neighbor? – then he may answer: "Yes, I keep peace." When asked again: Are you at peace with your neighbor in your feelings, in your sensations, thoughts, words and actions? – many a one who is of honest heart will beat on his breast. Maybe he will say: "Not always." Or he says: "I didn't see it this way before; I always thought I was at peace with my neighbor. Because I think well of my fellowman; I speak well of him, and my behavior is certainly in accordance with the commandments of God."

But what are the contents, the contents of your thoughts, of your words and your behavior, when seen as a whole? What are the contents of the five components: feeling, sensing, thinking, speaking and acting? This is what is decisive.

Oh see: You talk and talk and talk – do you really know what you are saying? You think and think and think – do you really know what you are thinking?

Oh recognize and grasp in your hearts: Are not many of the positive aspects that you attribute to yourselves, illusion? The one who believes that this world is the truth lives in illusion. The one who believes that his behavior corresponds to the truth lives in illusion.

Oh see and grasp in your hearts a picture: You are standing on the banks of a river. You look in the water and see the reflection of all that is on the riverbank, perhaps houses, bushes, trees, grass. When a compan-

ion now says to you: "Jump into the river and hold on to this tree!" – then you will say: "That's an illusion; that's only a reflection." And if you gather courage and jump into the water to hold onto the tree, then you see that it is impossible. Either you can swim or you sink. And so, there is nothing to hold onto in this reflection. It is similar with matter. Whatever you hold onto, a tree, a bush, a person, possessions – it is all mere illusion.

Oh see, the contents of your thoughts, your words, and actions are decisive, for these are energies that enter your soul and are stored there and in the corresponding repository planets. Your place of destination, which certainly is not pure chance, is also illusion. You can earn money by working; you acquire this and that. You work for possessions; you work for a so-called home, or you inherit from your parents, relatives or acquaintances. But what you possess – is this actually your property? Do you fill it out with the contents of your behavior? Or is it your property, your home, your place of destination, your money and possessions? Then you can be sure that this is illusion.

Many work for wealth, power and prestige; they bask in their illusion. For the one who is rich may be destitute in his soul. And the one who has acquired prestige may possibly not even be seen as a soul in the beyond. It is all illusion. If you bind yourself to people for the sake of your own advantage, then you will no longer find *them when you are in a soul garment. And so, it is illusion.*

Oh see: Whatever you hold onto in the way of matter, whether people, possessions, prestige, wealth, profit, inheritance and much more – it is all illusion.

What is fact? Fact, as seen by man, is far from the truth. Fact is what takes place in your five components, generally I call them patterns of behavior – that is what you store, that will be your places of destination after the death of your body. Do you know them? Few know them, for you hardly know yourselves, since you do not perceive the contents of these five components, that is, you live in the temporal and thus, in illusion.

Oh see, when your physical body passes away, your soul first goes to the in-between realms. The corresponding places of destination then call the soul, one after the other, as they become active in the soul. Do you know your place of destination? I say to you: If you do not come to know it here, on this side of life, then as a soul in the beyond you will be very disappointed. For the places of destination are seldom, very seldom, like your place of destination in the temporal. As a soul you will often be a stranger even in the beyond, because the places of destination look very different than those that you have acquired in the temporal through money, through possessions, through inheritance, through much more. And you will not know the souls that you meet there either, because you will still live in the illusion of your behavior patterns, which are not registered; instead, it is only their contents that are recorded. And since many souls continue to live in illusion, they work and work and work, to earn money and possessions, but they will earn nothing, because with the death of the body everything is over. Your profit or loss – you could also describe it as a mortgage, if it concerns your debt – you take with you as a soul into the beyond. And many a one will say: "Won't I be fetched by my acquaintances and relatives?" Perhaps. But your relatives, your acquaintances, your family, which you had in the temporal, will not be with you, for each family member recorded their inputs differently.

Man dies alone, and the soul goes alone to those places of destination in the beyond that it, as a human being through its patterns of behavior, has recorded. Every soul is accompanied by a guardian being, but often the souls hardly perceive the guardian beings, because they continue to live in illusion. And so, as a soul in the beyond you can neither earn nor buy – you have already recorded your earnings. Even when you still live in the illusion that you could – with death, everything is over. Many souls will hardly perceive the impulses from the guardian beings. Beings from higher regions that live in the planes of preparation, in order to prepare themselves for the pure Being, are often not heard either. The souls in the lower purification planes live in illusion, just as they lived when they were human beings; for as human beings they did not learn to recognize themselves *in* their five components, that is, in their ways of behavior.

Oh see: Many souls, and you know and experience this yourselves when you look at the world, are pressing to incarnate. Why? Because the magnetism is too strong. They are of the opinion that the flesh is the be-all and end-all; and the desire to experience this and that is often the path to incarnation. With the entry into an earthly existence, that is, with reincarnation, the cycle starts all over again. What was not cleared up by the soul in the beyond is taken with it as a whole into incarnation. As a human being, the soul carries everything from its former incarnations, everything that has not been paid off. From these previous incarnations, the components come together which then determine the life of the new person. And now it again depends on how the person thinks. Does he look into the contents of his ways of behavior, or does he just let the days go by and create further causes, that is, further incarnations?

If you consider your overpopulation, then you know how it may very well be in the beyond. In the beyond it is all about recognize and expiate. The expiation is often very, very sorrowful and very, very painful. The only help is to clear things up, to ask for forgiveness and to forgive. One cannot make amends there, because there is no matter there. Many souls do not forgive. Many incarnated souls, that is, people, also do not forgive. Magnets are in them that are oriented to the soul that suffers and endures pain in the beyond. These are the genes. The people send to the soul in the beyond which receives, because its inputs are active. What do such souls often do? Without looking more closely at the admonishing sensations, the images that are sent to them by the guardian beings, they go to incarnation. In the end, this occurs through procreation and birth; the body is available; the soul has come again and is now a human being. And now it is meant to clear things up with those people who are closest to this person. How this takes place in this world, you know yourselves: The other one is to blame for everything! This is – I take your words and use them – an even worse and more terrible cycle.

Oh see: The heavens are underway to enlighten the souls, but no guardian being will say: Go, O soul, to incarnation. If a guardian being were to say this, it would be bound to the soul, to everything that the person then more or less accomplishes in the temporal, for the guardian being would have taken the soul's freedom away. Every soul has its freedom in the beyond and *every person has his freedom – to record, record and record again, to create places of destination in the beyond and on this side of life. Who stands in-between? The Christ of God, who I Am, who calls and calls and calls: I Am the way, the truth and the life! I Am the redeeming power in you. Be aware of the Christ of God. Sanctify the commandments of God and the Sermon on the Mount, which I gave you. Become one with the commandments of God and the Sermon on the Mount, by walking the path to life and making peace with your neighbor, so that peace may grow in you and you may truly find your way into your inner being, to the eternal reality, for the Kingdom of God is the only reality, and it is in each one of you.*

No one comes to the Father except through Me, Christ, the Redeemer of all souls and men. Words. For many these are words – even for many of My brothers and sisters who think they are wise because of their technology.

So that you can understand better, here is a picture for you:
Every one of you who owns a so-called television set knows, and this is very logical to him, that in order to get a good picture he needs an appropriate antenna that must be adjusted to the station he wants to receive. But when it concerns seeing yourselves as a powerful

– I use your words – transmitting and receiving mast, which unceasingly transmits into the universe and receives in turn, then you shrug your shoulders and say: "Well, that may very well be."

But I say to you: With the contents of these five components, you transmit unceasingly. And according to the contents of these, your five components, you receive unceasingly. You send and receive. I ask you: Is it important how you call yourselves? Are your first and last names important to be able to receive the corresponding pictures? When you sit in front of your television sets, are your first and last names important? Is it important whether you call yourselves Original Christians, Christians, Moslems, Hindus and so much more, when you transmit, transmit and transmit what has nothing to do with your first and last names, nor with being Original Christian or Christian, or Moslem, Hindu or Buddhist? The one has nothing to do with the other.

Oh see: What happens when Original Christians or Christians orient themselves to the transmitter called the Church institution? Then they will receive rituals, ceremonies, church prayers, creeds and much more. Whether this is Original Christian or Christian does not matter – they receive what they are attuned to, that is, oriented to. But many so-called Christians, who have the path to life, which I Am, orient themselves to eastern meditation, to contemplating images. It does not matter whether you call yourselves Original Christian or Christian, whether you belong to a church institution or not – you will become what you send out, for you will receive it back again. This is what marks your consciousness, your subconscious, your cells, your soul. This is what goes into the repository stars, and after the death of your body you will suddenly belong to another religion. But in the temporal you called yourself Christian or Original Christian. The same holds true for a Moslem; no matter what religion, the name is not important – the sending potential is what is decisive. And just as he meditates and contemplates images, this is what he will become. If a Moslem practices Christian meditations, if he immerses into the nature kingdoms in the awareness of the great unity and the redeeming Spirit of the Christ of God, if he concerns himself with the contents of the Ten Commandments and the Ser mon on the Mount of Jesus more and more, then very gradually the Moslem will become a Christian.

To wherever you transmit, this is what you receive and what you become. A sage person, in earthly terms, talks about his technology; but when it concerns himself, he is blind. In this case, he is illogical.

My beloved brothers, My beloved sisters, I stand in-between and call. Now you have an inkling why the messengers of light make every effort with Me to radiate into the whole world the redeeming power, the true and genuine Christianity, the truth and the path to life. As Jesus, I promised to send the Comforter, who leads the people into the whole truth, insofar as they can understand it with human words. I have done this. I am doing it. And it is a great gift for the heavens that our sister is still a human being. As long as the body can be carried according to the laws of nature, the divine world will do this, in order to carry the truth, which I Am in the Father, into the whole world, in order to carry the path, which I Am, Christ, the redeeming power in souls and men, into the whole world and to build up the atmosphere of the Christ-of-God, for there was never such a turn of time as you are now experiencing. This turn of time is moving slowly, very slowly toward the end of this sinful world.

I come. And I come with My own, in whom I can resurrect. Beloved brother, can I resurrect in you? Beloved sister, can I resurrect in you? In your thoughts, in your words, in your actions, in your feelings and sensations – can I resurrect in you? Then come, and follow Me! For I Am establishing the Kingdom of Peace, since I Am the truth and the life. For the earth must be cleansed, and the earth-soul must be released, because in it is the radiation of the eternal Jerusalem.

My kingdom is not of this world. If your kingdom is of this world, then you do not know yourself. And if you do not know yourself, you do not know Me. How dismal it will be one day, when the hour strikes ...

But I call My own. I call My own to proceed with the cleansing of the temple with My help, with the great grace and kindness of God, so that the soul, too, may cleanse itself and attune itself to God, to the infinitely eternal transmitter of light of the I Am, in order to receive from Him. This is why I struggle, why I fight for this, with the power of the Father's love, in whom I Am.

I fight for every person! I fight for every soul! Feel this in the prophetic words. However, you remain free to choose: illusion or truth.

I will not turn away from any human being or soul. I go after all of you, and even if it is in the deepest depths, for I Am in the Father and the Father is in Me. The **one** Spirit is love – He loves you. Do you feel the longing of the heavens to know that all of you are in the heavens of the Being, including the many, many people in this world, the countless souls in the spheres of purification? Everywhere suffering, everywhere pain, everywhere torment and strife, quarrelling, hatred, envy – and always "my neighbor is to blame." It can't keep going on like this. The one who is not with his brother, with his sister, in his thoughts, in his words, in his feelings, is against Me.

I love you. All people, all souls, make up the great flock, and I Am the shepherd. I go after each one. Happy the one who joins Me, who follows Me, who goes with Me, in order to gather those who are calling, who are standing by the wayside, who need help and salvation – also through you. And as it becomes a great host of love, more and more hosts of the heavens will join this host of love, will join the people, and fight with them in love for peace, and the Kingdom of Peace will emerge with those who bear peace in their hearts.

And so, feel: I Am with you, the Good Shepherd, who is the way, the truth and the life.

Peace.

Let It Become As It Is In Heaven!

Christ Revelation, 1987

*Y*ou are from Me and I Am in you. My power is your life and My love comes to you, My brother, My sister. In these earthly minutes during which I reveal Myself in word, I come to you as your brother, not only as your Redeemer. Yes, I want to consciously be your brother and walk with you.

Many of you believe that the Father and I, His Son, your brother, are far away.

My brothers and sisters, our spirit bodies are fine-material – of another aggregate state, the highest cosmic vibration, which material eyes that are attuned to the earthly vibration do not see. However, the spiritual eyes of the one who journeys to the kingdom of the inner being are opened, and in the kingdom they behold the only king of the heavens and of this earth, God, our Father.

In the kingdom of the inner being, you behold your brother and friend, Christ, and there, in the realm of the inner being, you behold the beings of light. Oh feel in these minutes that we are not far from you, for heaven *encompasses this earth and enfolds every single one of you. Yes, heaven, the essence of infinity, of everything beautiful, pure, noble and fine, is in you, thus, it is so near! Heaven breathes through you. Heaven is love; it is power; it is life, and every breath taken is life. The life, the breath in your breathing, flows from the heavens, from your inner being. There, in your inner being, everything that is beautiful and pure, noble, good, yes, perfect, can be seen.*

The Father and I and the beings of light are not far from you. You feel distant only when you direct your senses, your human thinking and striving to without, where the earthly attractions disturb the senses. Through this, your connection to God, to the inner senses, is also disturbed, and you think that only what can be grasped by the outer senses is reality. But the one who journeys inward, senses that heaven is near.

And so, I, your brother, radiate the Inner Path. What does the Inner Path mean?

The Inner Path is the path to the heart of God. Everyone begins by examining and monitoring his thoughts. Replace the human, negative thoughts – thoughts of hatred, envy, animosity, discord, strife and much more – with positive thoughts, thoughts of selfless love, thoughts of peace, of hope, of confidence and faith. Then the sullen, doubting, spiteful and derogatory thoughts will fade away. You receive much more light through positive thoughts, and it is then also possible for you to recognize everything that is active in your consciousness and subconscious, perhaps from the past, and to overcome it by the power of inner love. Your worldly desires no longer compel your senses to without. You will fulfill your smaller desires as they fit your present conditions, and take pleasure in them.

In this way, your willfulness, too, will subside, and this willfulness, the base little ego, is replaced by the divine will, which says: "The Father's will shall be done. Father, show me what is good!" And the One who dwells in you and constantly knocks at your door will, by way of sensations and feelings, reveal to you what His will is.

Suddenly you will feel: Why should I be hostile toward my neighbor? I will take the first step now; I will go to him and ask for forgiveness, even though I thought until now that he should come to me and ask me for forgiveness. You take the first step and then feel a sense of freedom. You have let go. The Father in you guided you, and now you feel peace and you emit this peace. Your neighbor, toward whom you harbored animosity, is now consciously your brother, your friend.

This encouragement from your inner being brings further steps. You clear up your past; you let go of what you had bound yourself to, for example, that your neighbor should think and act as you want. Free will says: Your neighbor is also a child of God and is bur-

dened in a different way than you are. He still must take this or that step in order to find the path, the direct path, to the heart of God. This was the will of God in you. Let go and be a friend and brother, be a sister, to your neighbor, be a child of God, and you will let go, while realizing: "Yes, he or she has free will. I may not boss my neighbor around or force **my** will upon him."

If you follow the fine, subtle sensations of your inner being, then the selfless, impersonal love will awaken more and more in you and you will feel peace and joy. You will feel an inspiring and free feeling; it is the light of the Father in Me, the Christ. Your consciousness expands and you see the world with totally different eyes. You feel that the world needs liberation and that so many people live in the chains of their human ego, that they are enslaved by their own ego. You see need, illness, infirmity and much more. What will you do?

You will feel the will of God, a gentle urging in you, which wants to tell you: My child, take the next step toward divine wisdom, toward the divine deed. Bring justice to this world, for justice shall prevail over right. All people and beings who feel God in themselves are united in this justice. – And you will take the first step; and the deed, the wisdom of God, awakens in you. The divine flows into your sensations and feelings and wants to say to you: Oh see, the eternal law of love says: "Pray and Work." The right work is like the right prayer; it is a lawful life. You recognize the servitude of the people in external, worldly enterprises. You see how many are unhappy and desperate, because they are pressured from "above," as you say. They "must" – and "may" not.

Many people are exploited, and yet they are children of God, equipped with a free will. You suddenly realize that the Inner Path, the path to the heart of God, is not meant just for the individual, not just for your own unfoldment. On the level of Wisdom, of the deed, you feel that now you may draw from your inner being. Yes, you can do it; you have experience in overcoming your human ego. And you feel the urge to help the inner kingdom, to which you are so near, to grow and develop externally. You feel in you that dominating people, superiors and subordinates should not exist. You feel in you that nations and races should not exist. You feel the cosmic life in you and sense infinity and the heavenly beings as **one** people, **one** love in God, our Father. What you feel, what vibrates and lives in you, urges you to help it become visible externally. See, My brother, see, My sister, more and more are walking on this path; and many are urged by the inner light, the homeland of the inner being: Let it become as it is in heaven! – My brother, my sister, oh see, the heavenly beings do not just float from heaven to heaven, where there are only fine-material streams. In every heaven there are dwelling places, spiritual structures, where the families do not live shut off from each other. Instead, since everything is one unity, they form the great family in God, our Father, who is, at the same time, our Mother.

The spirit beings in heaven are active according to their mentality. God, the eternal light, the eternal primordial power, breathes in and out continuously – in and out. The primordial power breathes in a mighty eon cycle – in and out. Thus, spiritual evolution is unceasing, yes, constant. From one spiritual atom, spiritual manifestations are again issued, and the beings of light are active everywhere, where there are new formations of creation, where evolution continues, where more suns and worlds have developed, where spirit children mature through the inner power and grow into spirit beings. The beings of light are constantly in action. They do not create and work with this speed, with this hectic activity, like man, but embedded in the cosmic rhythm of unending love. This is the fulfillment of the eternal law; this is the worship of God.

And My brothers and sisters in the earthly garment, who feel this inner glory, this inner creation of the beings of light – stimulated by My Spirit, they strive to accomplish similar things, of course, in matter, with different possibilities, with other forms and the like. But what radiates into these different possibilities and forms of the three-dimensional world is what the homeland is: peace, love, harmony.

Dear brother, dear sister, the Inner Path does not exist merely to think about personal aspects; these are the first steps: Recognize yourself, and clear up what you have recognized. But further along on the path, the consciousness opens for many people, yes, for all people and souls. Then it is: One for all and all for One.

And so, dear brothers and sisters, you experience the first path. The Father spoke of the first step toward the actualization of what is an urging in one's inner being: the Kingdom of God on this earth.
Dear brothers and sisters, you are children of a king. Our Father, the king, the Regent of the heavens, does not want to see His own in need, living in caves, sick and suffering, the victims of infirmity, being spiteful or angry. He wants to awaken them through Me and show them: Walk the path and you will experience in your heart what many already experience in themselves, the Kingdom of God also in the material existence.

My brothers and sisters, the Kingdom of Peace was already announced, long ago. My heart flows to every one of you and to the many who are not present during these minutes: Join in! Walk the path – at first to experience yourself and to clear up many things, and then to be there for the many who will still come and who will form the future generations. Surely, many of you will be there again; for what you experience now, in this incarnation, in your heart, deep in your inner being, you will bring with you into this world again. It will radiate from you and you will continue to create and build, for you, for your fellow brothers and sisters, and not lastly, with and for your brother, Christ. These are outer activities, not in the spirit of this world, but in the spirit of the inner being and according to the Kingdom of God, which want to become active in your inner being and want to be manifest externally.

Oh see and experience in your inner being and through the explanations of our brothers and sisters how it should be, the first steps, the first path. And be understanding, because as you have heard, in many of My own a process of turning inside out is taking place – and thus, in each one of you, who strive to do the will of the Father, from the human toward the spiritual. Here and there, what is human still comes through; the individual may recognize it and clear it up through My power. Just as I, and above all the Father through Me, are greatly understanding of all of you, so you, too, be understanding with each other.

And I ask you to let love stream out of the understanding for each other, selfless love. Love one another as I have loved My own as Jesus, and love My own as Christ. Love each other from the heart and fulfill the holy laws of love, of peace and harmony, and with alert hearts you will experience more and more what is gradually opening up: the Kingdom of God on this earth. And above everything hovers the Spirit, who pulsates in the hearts and penetrates the earth.

Love one another as I love you. And adhere to the glorious awareness: freedom, unity, brotherliness in the Spirit of your brother, Christ.

Do You Speak the Language of Love?

Christ Revelation, 1996

My peace and My love I bring to you. I Am Christ, your Redeemer and Brother. Look deeply into the words of life and grasp the meaning of My words, and you will learn to sense your eternal homeland.

My peace I bring to you.
What do these words want to tell you? I bring you My peace. Why do I bring you My peace? Because many live in discord. Yes, the whole world is restless.

My kingdom is a kingdom of peace and a kingdom of love. This kingdom – your, our, divine heritage – dwells in you. Look into the words, that the kingdom of love and peace dwells in you. Have you entered this kingdom? Then you speak the language of this kingdom, the language of love.

My kingdom, which is not of this world, is a kingdom of beauty, of unending splendor, abundance, clarity, harmony, a kingdom of all-pervading radiation. The one who lives in this kingdom speaks the language of love.

Do you speak the language of love? If yes, then there is no need for prophets. But My entire striving is to teach all of you – all who are willing – the language of the eternal homeland, more and more, the language of love, so that the Spirit no longer has need of prophets; instead you yourselves will be spirit of My Spirit, conscious beings of light, beings of the Spirit, who speak the language of love.

*Now look **into** your thoughts, not only **at** your thoughts. Look into your thoughts and ask yourselves the question: Are they noble? Are they pure? Are your thoughts like the sounds of the language of love? Look deeply into the life of your feelings. Are your feelings, the life of your feelings, the same as the language of love?*

Many a one will shrug his shoulders and think: "One day, It will be like that." It will happen one day, that is correct. But is it right when you, O brother, O sister, know that you should not feel or think in this way? It will be one day – but when? It is you, who decide. But what lies in the time in-between until it has come so far? That which you have input, or stored, through your feeling, sensing, thinking, speaking and acting.

Many a one will again shrug his shoulders and say to himself: "I have been thinking the way I want to for a long time and I am fine. I have been talking the way I want to for a long time and I am fine. What I do has brought and brings me success – and I am fine."

Oh recognize that you record everything that you sense, feel, think and speak in the storage system of the two cosmos, the material cosmos and the cosmos of the purification planes, and not least, in your soul, but also in your subconscious, and your consciousness carries a part of it, as well. The cosmos move; stars and planets form. If a constellation carries your inputs, if they become active in it, then they come to light. And one day it happens: Fate has caught up with you. Why? Because you speak your sinful language. With this your language, you add to the structure of your fate. At the same time, you know that in the atmosphere there is the so-called atmospheric chronicle, where the thoughts of all people from all times are recorded. When thoughts of the same and similar kind are formed, if they are stimulated by people who think the same and similar things, then they rain down, so to speak, and seize those who have a share in them.

How often do you say: "This or that one acted against the earthly law. He deceived. He stole from his neighbor. He said untrue things about him, slandering and discriminating against him. Yes, this or that one even committed murder." You say, **they** are the ones. I ask you: Aren't you also a part of this? Examine your thoughts.

Hatred, envy, animosity, discord, destruction, greed and much more is thought and thought and thought by man. Passions mark him. Much of this goes into the *atmospheric chronicle. Like forces gather and rain down, as it were. An unstable person then carries out the deed that has gathered in the atmospheric chronicle and has become active. He is the culprit. Who is the abettor? Oh, ask yourself!*

Examine your words. Examine your thoughts, your feelings, your passions – all of them are components that come together as pictures, also in the atmospheric chronicle, which in many cases needs only a slight prod, and they come down and stimulate this or that person to talk badly, to commit evil deeds. He is the culprit. Where are the abettors?

Oh recognize that in many cases you have a share in this. All this, every little quantum, every nuance of your feeling, thinking, speaking and acting is weighed, measured and justly recorded, also in both cosmos. Oh see, how much is written in you. It is written in your consciousness, in your subconscious, in your cells, your soul; much is in the atmospheric chronicle, and every nuance is written in both cosmos.

Today you are living in prosperity. And so, the question arises: Where does the prosperity come from, the abundance, as it were, for you? Does it come from the divine language, because you speak the language of love in your feelings, sensations, thoughts, words and actions? Or where does this contentment, this satiation, for many prosperity, come from? What do you emit? Who lets himself be caught and serves you?

Oh see, many, many stumbling blocks, many, many traps. And you do not know them! Many a one shrugs his shoulders, saying: "It will be one day." Yes, it will be one day that you, O human child, will speak the language of love. Will you accept everything that lies in-between? Your egoistic language that brings you only bad things, that brings you worries and needs, where you do not know what can happen in the next hours, in the next days – will you accept all of this? I speak into the conscience of each one. O brother, O sister, will you accept this?

If you want to speak your primordial language, the language of love – know and experience in your heart that God, the love, **cannot** *turn away from you, from any person, from any soul. Look into these words: God, the love, cannot turn away from you, because God, the eternal Father, loves you. Even if you have a destructive effect on your body, if you burden your soul – God does not turn away from you. It is not possible for Him to turn away from you, because He is the love, which always gives and always, at every moment, eternally, speaks to you. But with your sinful thoughts, words and deeds, with all your negative inputs, you turn away from God. But God does not turn away from you – He is giving, always giving. However, realize that the giving Spirit of the eternal Father in Me, Christ, your Redeemer, dwells in you. He beholds you. He knows about your doings – and does not turn away from you.*

Oh recognize that it often means Golgotha for Me, when I touch you and you shrug your shoulders and say: "It will be one day." When, from the depths, from the very depths of your soul, I whisper to you: Brother, sister, do not think this way! Do not add on to the structure of your fate. Come, turn back! And you shrug your shoulders, saying: "It will be one day."

*Feel very gently into the power of the redemption, into the Christ of God, who brought everything as Jesus on Golgotha, so that you can turn back **now**, and not someday. Feel into the Christ of God, whether the stigmata do not hurt over and over again, when you shrug your shoulders and say: "It will be one day."*

*See, I live with you, because I Am in you. I feel with you because I love you. I call you from the very basis of your soul, and you do not hear Me. I ask you to turn back, because you are children of the fullness, children of the love. And you shrug your shoulders and say: "It will be one day." Are not these often pinpricks or nails in My heart? Cannot the lance be felt again and again? I dwell in you. I walk with you. I Am always **for you**! The Spirit of God, the one Spirit in the Father, Father and Son, in the one power of the one Spirit, is always for you. It is not possible for Him to turn away from you, because He loves you infinitely. And you still want to wait, to wait, until you speak the language of love?*

Oh feel, feel into your heart. Feel deeply into it, in order to there fathom how near I Am to each one of you. Verily, I Am always present. I always give love. I always send peace. I always offer My help. I Am always present for you, My brother, for you, My sister.

If you are for Me, then you are for yourself, for your inner being, for your true life. And then, you will dismantle the structure of your fate and you will feel free. Do you know what freedom means? You will feel this only when you speak the language of love; for it is clarity; it is beauty; it is purity; it is the symmetrical balance of all things. It streams throughout space and time and soars into eternity, all-irradiating, because the language of love is the law of love. The language of love is caring, loving. The language of love is the constant communication with the One, who Himself is the love, with the law, with infinity, with everything pure. This is freedom. This is grace. This is beauty. This is clarity. This results in the fullness – you will never live in need. Then your prosperity is humble, for the fullness is the true wealth, the treasure of infinity.

You, you, you – each and every one is a great treasure of infinity. When, brother, when, sister, will you fulfill your divine heritage in the language of love?

Begin to speak the language of love. Believe. Trust. Surrender yourself to Me, and know: The great love can never turn away from you, because it is always eternally giving. It, the love, which loves you, always sees you in the heart of love. And this is how the love is active. This is how the love gives – always the best for your soul, so that it may become love again.

Let My words reverberate in your hearts. And become aware that I Am always and eternally present, always for you, for each one. In this awareness, go within. Feel deeply into My words, into what touched you, and ask yourself: When shall it be?

My peace and My love I leave with you,
your brother and Redeemer, Christ.

The World Talks About Peace. Where Is the Peace?

God-Father Revelation, 1988

I Am your Lord and God, you shall have no other gods before Me. In the sign of redemption, where does man stand? Does he stand next to My Son, whom I sent to mankind, so that it could become as I have beheld and created it – divine?

What are your gods? Even though you pray with your lips to one God – it is the Mammon; it is the external things of this world, wealth, prestige – egocentricity in countless variations. The majority of my children pray, but where is the fulfillment of the prayer? Look into your world and, ultimately, look at yourselves.

Many say: Christ, Christ, You, my Redeemer! What do you surrender to your Redeemer? You pray and pray; but you should put into practice what you pray to your Redeemer, so that you may become as I have beheld and created you and that you may again behold My countenance as children of your Father, who I Am.

How long will you still speak of the Spirit and not become spirit of My Spirit? How long will you still speak of love for God and not become love of My love?

How long will you still read the gospels in your Bibles and not live according to them?

You obscure what was and is sent to you: the prophets – and thus, My word and that of My Son. Many among you are hypocrites; they affirm God's love, but that is all they do. Where is their basis? Where is the basis of all those who call themselves representatives of the life? If they were representatives of the life, they would be children of God, one unity in the Spirit of their Redeemer.

What do your denominations consist of? Solely of the earthly claim to power. For if they had the spirit of truth, then many on earth would be inspired by the truth and prophecy would no longer be needed, for then My own would be My word. Instead, they are elusory people who go along with the attitudes of those who strive solely for might and prestige on this earth.

In this way, Christ is denied day after day, hour after hour, minute after minute. And in this way, doubt is sown about the eternal Spirit, who I Am, the life from eternity to eternity.

My children shall find their way out of need and tribulation. This is why I sent My Son, who became your Redeemer. But where are the first steps of My children toward their Redeemer? Many speak of Him, but their steps go into the world. Power, prestige, pos-

sessions and chattel are the Mammon, the gods, that is, the idols. Where is the love, the warmth among the people, which Jesus of Nazareth radiated? Where is the fellowship of nations that Jesus wanted? Where is the harmony in the hearts of the people? Covered over with vain delusions!

Oh recognize and grasp in your hearts: I am calling directly to you and I am calling you via Christ to turn back! To where? Not to someone who promises salvation, but to your hearts, for I dwell there, since you are the temple of My Spirit. And I admonish you not to believe what I say here either; I admonish you to actualize what you believe in, be it selfless love, be it inner peace, be it inner harmony.

The one who merely speaks is not close to God. But the one who actualizes draws closer to the heart of life and senses My word in himself.

My children, you are still human beings, but in you is the radiating life from Me. What happens when you leave the temporal, the material body? Do you think that the heavens will open up and you will be in the sanctum of your Father? At the moment your physical eyes close, you change only the scene, but you are the same. Your baggage is not clothing, shoes, money and possessions; in the fine-material regions of the beyond your baggage is what you have written into your souls:

hatred, envy, hostility, strife – or selfless love, harmony and peace. What you are now sowing in your thoughts at these moments goes into your souls; this is what you are yourselves, and this is your baggage. You will go with it through the veils of consciousness and awaken as souls and recognize what clings to you.

Again and again you hear the words: Make use of the hours; make use of the minutes. Words are merely terms, but when you grasp the content of the words, then you will grasp what grace the earth possesses. For the unending love, which I Am, radiates grace onto this earth, into this world. Grace is the same as protection and guidance for all those who try to take the step toward Christ in their inner being.

Oh see, your human thoughts are visible to a person only when he is enlightened. For a person still on the path to enlightenment, your thoughts are not visible. But thought is power and energy. And if your thoughts flow to those who strive to walk the path within, grace starts working to protect these pilgrims on the way to the consciousness of love, so that they take in only as much of the negative forces, as is good for their soul in serving its further development. But in the regions of the beyond, behind the veils of consciousness, everything is apparent. There, grace is not effective, because you see it yourselves and experience it in your spirit bodies. There, Redemption indeed continues to be effective as the pulsating power that shows you the way out of what you experience and see in your soul bodies. For there everything is apparent, each thought, each sensation, the word of the person, the deed.

Oh recognize which consciousness you live in. You live in the consciousness of grace, if you take the first steps out of the human ego via the actualization of the eternal laws.
Everyone is given the opportunity to find his way out of tribulation and need; this is why the redemption is in each and every one of you. But you, My child, have to nourish the Redeemer-flame, by giving it your human aspects, so that they may be transformed and you may receive ever more divine power.

I said to you that many prayers are not fruitful. Why not? Because they are not inspired by the love for Me. Oh see, I Am Spirit, omnipresent, eternally streaming Spirit. Your free will is based on the fact that I touch you with My Spirit, but do not pressure you to think, live and act in a spiritual way. Just as the sun does not pressure you to absorb its rays. It shines. It does not pressure you to go out of the shade into the light; it does not pressure you to go out of the cellar into the brightness; it does not pressure you to open your windows and doors – it shines. And this is how I shine.

Only those who develop selflessness communicate with selflessness, with Me, the Spirit. Every pure, selfless thought is the same as communication with Me, the Spirit. Every human thought, in turn, communicates with what is human. What a person sows is what he will reap; therein lies the communication. You cannot move a finger unless the Spirit gives you the strength for it. Strength is the same as communication, when the person moves, when he sees, hears, smells, tastes and touches. The pure Being is purest communication with Me, the All-Spirit, the Father-Mother-God. And if you live in the causal law, the law of sowing and reaping, you communicate unceasingly with your own thoughts, words and actions, that you have sent out into the atmosphere, that surround you, and which you call up, according to your feeling, thinking, speaking and acting.

And so, when you merely pray and your prayer is not inspired by love, by selfless love, you do not communicate with the highest powers of love. This is why your prayers are not fruitful.

My child, what did Jesus of Nazareth call upon you to do? To actualize the Sermon on the Mount! What does the Christ, your Redeemer, offer you? To recognize the Sermon on the Mount in the details of life, to put it into practice, for this is the way to the kingdom of the inner being.

You say you cannot walk this path? You cannot? – You do not want to! Why? Because the Mammon fosters you. But if you recognize who you are, you will experience how low the human ego is, how your own ego enslaves you. You are afraid of the future – why? Can it be because you are in servitude to your own thoughts and senses?

Oh see and grasp, My children, the path leading out of the servitude to the human ego is again offered to you. For good reason, My child, only offered! In this you recognize that I do not pressure you. I do not influence you. I shine. And if you take the first step toward selflessness, you will find ever more access to the great, pure, all-encompassing communication with the positive energies of life, with Me, the Spirit of your Father.

Even though My words are earnest, you recognize in them the hope for you, the peace for you, the harmony for you and the all-encompassing selfless love for you. Do not say "for others." For you! For when you have become the instrument of My love, then you radiate My love and can inspire your neighbor.

Oh recognize, the world talks about peace. Where is the peace? Many talk about harmony. Is the harmony in them? The Christians talk about Christ. Is He consciously risen in them? Many talk about Me, the Father-Mother-God – and their hearts are filled with fear and worry!

Is this the world that carries its Redeemer? Do not say that the other one should do it! **You** *are called to carry your Redeemer, Christ, consciously in you. This means to place each thought on the scales of the law and to weigh whether it is divine or egoistic. And if it is egoistic, surrender it to your Redeemer, Christ in you. For He dwells in you, in order to consume what is human, to let you become divine again, just as I have beheld and created you.*

And if you consciously and joyfully take the first step to your Redeemer, by weighing your thoughts, your words, your inclinations and stirrings, by bringing them to your Redeemer and no longer doing them, you will sense My holy grace, which protects and vivifies you, and you will securely take the first steps on the path to the inner life.

Rejoice and feel, My child, that the Spirit of love dwells in you, and your inner being is immortal. Do you know when you will leave your human shell? For this reason, be alert, every moment, every hour, every day. Remember the inner scales: Weigh your life, and take the steps toward Christ, who dwells in you.

And if you can grasp the meaning of My words, then you recognize that I do not lead you to any denomination. I do not lead you to any outer religion. I do not lead you to any person to whom you should listen. I lead you into the kingdom of the inner being, to your

Redeemer. And the guidance is in each thought that you weigh; the guidance is in each word, in each action, for in everything Am I, the power of life. Weigh your thoughts, whether they are selfless or based on human aspects, and you will recognize your path, and ultimately, you will recognize yourself.

Weigh your words. Do they correspond to your thoughts? Or do you merely pretend to be what you are not? Then hurry up to find what is selfless in this, and act accordingly. Then you will recognize your path. Weigh your deeds, whether they are selfless or egoistic, and act quickly. Go to your Lord **in you**; surrender your human aspects and you will recognize the path of love **in you**. And you will no longer be lonesome, because you will find your way to people of like mind, who likewise struggle with their human ego, who shed things, and journey into the heart of love, which I Am.

Oh recognize the freedom that radiates to you. Just as you now, at this moment, think, this is what you are. What do you want to do with your thoughts? Just as you now, at this moment, feel, this is what you are. What do you want to do with your feelings? Do you want to take them to Christ or to betray Him, by thinking in a human way again, by directing your steps to without again?

My child, I Am the justice. Everything is weighed, measured – what impression will you make and how will you be evaluated? Do not say that there is still time. The opportunity is given to you now, to recognize and find yourself now.

Life lasts eternally, because I Am eternal. And since you are from Me, your spiritual body will be eternal. But when will you enter the glory, your homeland? When you are pure, flawless! Therefore, make use of the time, make use of every moment, ask for forgiveness and forgive, and sin no more. This is a large aspect on the path within. Find the good in your neighbor, affirm it, and you will develop yourself into the good. For as soon as you come into communication with the positive powers, you become clear and alert and recognize immediately when the darkling creeps up, in order to lead you astray in your sensations and thoughts, yes, also with words and actions.

My child, I Am calling you! Your Redeemer, My Son, opened the heavens for you. The gates are open. Enter your eternal homeland, I, your Father, await you. But you will pass through the gate into the eternal homeland, to your eternal dwelling place, only when you nourish the Redeemer-flame, by surrendering to the flame the human aspects that you have recognized, and thus, receive strength from the Christ-power.

And so, what do you want to do? You cannot destroy yourself. And if you destroy your body, you remain as *the soul of the human being with everything that has not been cleared up. And recognize that the grace helps you to clear up everything, before you have to experience it on your body. Your thoughts, your feelings, your words and actions, look into them. They tell you what you should clear up now, so that the waves of your human ego do not hit your body and you have to suffer. For you are the suffering yourself, the need, the illness, the poverty, because you have acted against the inner wealth.*

But look to your Redeemer in you. You should not suffer. You should not be poor. You should not be sick. He gives you impulses beforehand, and they are: Turn back, My child, turn back in your feelings, thoughts, words and actions, in your stirrings and inclinations, turn back! Here you encounter your brother and your sister. What are you thinking? Ask for forgiveness and forgive, and do it from your heart. Yes, My child, do it from your heart, for what is not done from your inner being, remains in you and clings to you, and you will experience and see it, at the latest, when you have left this body. For this reason, make use of the time, and transform it within yourself toward eternity, for you are a child of eternity.

Transform the time, My child, by thinking cosmically. To think cosmically means to be connected to the pure Being. To live cosmically means to live with your neighbor in peace and concordance. To love cosmically means to meet your neighbor selflessly, to give and to expect nothing. And so, live cosmically, and you will live universally, for then, the borders will fall away, and it will be **one** people, the people of Christ. My Son, your Redeemer, leads you there, all people, all souls.

You have come here, into this worldly structure, voluntarily, and just as you have come, you can go again. You do not need to accept a word from My Spirit. I radiate My love to you. If you accept it, you will become rich in your inner being. If you doubt, this is also good. If you smile at it, this is also good. If you reject My word, this is also in order – for you. But I continue to radiate into all eternity. Through this, My child, you will find your way back to Me. When? I leave up to you, because you have your free will. The law that you have created through your human ego has its effect on you. Liberate yourself from it, and then you will find your way into the cosmic Being and be in communication with Me, the Spirit of your Father. And you will live in glory, in peace and selfless love with Me, your Father from eternity to eternity.

That Am I, the Spirit from eternity to eternity, and you are, whether you want to accept it or not, My child from eternity to eternity.

Where Do You Stand?
At My Right Hand?

Christ Revelation, 1991

I Am in God, My Father, Christ, His Son. The Father is greater than I. For this reason, the Son and the divine Wisdom bow before His glory and greatness.

The time is near in which I will take over the rulership of the earth and of all the spheres of purification, together with the divine Wisdom.

My Father is greater than I. I Am the omnipresent power in God, in the first four basic powers of life, also called the natures of God. God, our eternal Father, is the All-power, that is, omnipresent. He is power, love, wisdom. He is the whole of infinity. He is the Father-Mother-God. He is the life of the children.

Eternal, glorious Father, your Son thanks You, that You sent Me to bring the power of redemption to Your children. Eternal, glorious Father, all of infinity bows before You; all Being is in Your service.

You great All-One, you mighty, eternal Primordial Spirit, Your love is unending, powerful and wise. I thank You from My heart that I can be active on earth and in the spheres of purification for Your fallen and burdened children. You gave Me the strength to bring redemption, and, at the same time, You protect the potential of the redemptive power.

Eternal, glorious Father, I, Your Son, thank You. I took on all human beings and souls as My adoptive children. This is why I address them in Your name as My children. For I lead them out of tribulation, need, illness and pain, to You, You who are from eternity to eternity.

Eternal, glorious Father, our kingdom is the bliss, the beauty, the splendor from You. You are the shining Absolute Law, which is imperishable, because You are absolute and perfect. So Am I in You, in Your absoluteness and perfection, spirit of Your Spirit, omnipresent in the four basic powers of Your life, and thus, omnipresent in all human beings and souls.

Glorious Father, Your will is done.

My children, My beloved brothers and sisters in the Spirit of My Father, the homeland, the eternal Being, is radiating, shining, absolute power. Your eternal home is there, the homeland of the pure spirit beings. I lead you there. And the primordial power of the Father will transform everything impure; and the primordial *power will bring everything into the radiating, eternally shining, eternal law, God.*

The eternal law is unchangeable; and those who live in the eternal law are compressed spiritual-divine law. And so, the pure law, the Absolute Law, has no influence on the pure beings; the pure beings are compressed law themselves, and are in constant communication with the absolute, divine Being, the eternal law.

Just as in heaven, so is the communication on earth, too, yes, in the whole of infinity. All forces communicate with each other; this also results in gravity. Everything carries; everything moves; there is no standstill, for God is life.

When the Fall began, God gave a part of the primordial law into the law of sowing and reaping, that is, a potential of divine energy. God said to His children: I give you a part of My primordial power. No matter where you are, no matter where you move or what you do, you have your free will. You can transform the spiritual potential down, transform it into your law through your wrong way of thinking and acting – or you can bring it back. But it is written in the primordial law: You will bring the whole potential in again one day. And if you transform it into negative energy, you will transform it back up again, into pure cosmic energy.

The Fall-beings took the potential of cosmic energy and transformed it down. As a result, the law of sowing and reaping developed. All further beings, who burdened themselves, kept transforming the law down and it became the so-called causal law. The souls lost ever more spiritual power, and so, the primordial life supplied the next potential; it is the Redeemer-power, a large part of My spiritual heritage. This spiritual heritage cannot be transformed down; it is divided up into sparks, that are in every soul. This is the Redeemer-deed. This took place on Golgotha; it was inherent in the "It is finished." By virtue of this Redeemer-potential, you will find your way back again into the eternal kingdom of love and peace.

Oh see, everyone is now given the opportunity, to turn back now, at this moment, to give the negative to the redeeming and liberating light, thus growing into the divine-eternal law. The one who does not strive for this now, the one who takes his time, will not be punished by God – he punishes himself.

You have heard from our eternal Father that everything is based on communication. The pure beings communicate with the eternal, pure Being, the impure beings with what they have sent into the world and into the astral worlds.

Every feeling, every thought, every word and every action is energy. No energy is lost. The positive as well as the negative energy flows back to the sender. The positive energies are selfless, loving feelings, thoughts, words and actions, and, in the soul and person, they bring about freedom and the ascent into higher spheres of life, yes, all the way to the Absoluteness, into the divine Being. The negative energies also come back to soul and person, because everything is communication. Even when you are simply afraid of something means that a communication exists with forces that you sent out either in this life or in one of your former lives. And so, fear is a sign that wants to tell you: Turn back! Trust!

Every thought of hatred, of envy, shows you: Turn back! Love selflessly; accept your neighbor – before you reinforce the forces that you have sent out, and which will then break in over you. The signs that you receive are manifold, before you are hit by what you have sent out yourself. If you are alert and clear up in time what you have recognized, then the negative will transform into positive power, and you will climb higher on the ladder to the cosmic Being.

My child, our Father said: Make use of the time! And thus speaks your Redeemer, as well: Make use of the time and recognize yourself in every thought, and also recognize in time the hint of fate. For the grace of God prevails and shows you beforehand what could perhaps hit you. The signs show this in fear, in anxiety, in doubt, hatred, envy, in all human aspects. Know that what a person sows is what he will reap. But *provided he repents in time and no longer sins, the negativity transforms into positive energy, and the harvest does not have to be borne or has to be borne only in part, depending on how large the negative potential is, and if this is good for the soul.*

Thus, everything is taken into consideration in the great law of life. You are not lost! You are recognized in all details. You are yourself in the great book of life, in the law of sowing and reaping and in the Absolute Law, and everything is registered in your soul.

My child, what will happen if you now, at this moment, leave the temporal? The eternal Father said: Your soul goes through the veils of consciousness, there, where your physical eye cannot see. The Father said that you change only the scene, yet as a soul you remain the same person.

Oh see, when you go to sleep, the soul separates from the body, and when you awaken again, you speak of dreams. But in the end, you do not know where the soul was. And yet, it was underway, perhaps it penetrated the veils of consciousness and looked around at where its spiritual place of destination is, according to its state of development.

The soul returns, but the information received from the soul by the person is sparse – perhaps a dream, perhaps only an inkling that the soul was here and there.

Why can the soul not specifically convey to the person where it was? Because the person, the external shell, is tied to the temporal, to the three dimensions. But as soon as the soul leaves its house, its body, further dimensions awaken in it.

My children, My beloved brothers and sisters, life lasts eternally and no child is lost. No child should have to bear what so very many people bear – suffering, hardship, illness, fate and much more.

A great number of people say: "The other one is to blame for my fate, for my illness." Who is the other one? It is the one whom you do not want to accept, namely, your neighbor. "The other one is to blame!" Accept the other one as your neighbor! He is not to blame for your illness, for your suffering. He was perhaps a mirror for you in a quarrel and in many a conversation. Do not say "The other one irritated me, this is why I have this condition." The other one is your neighbor. He was a mirror for you. You hardly saw it because you did not look into the mirror. You did not notice what your neighbor unconsciously wanted to say to you, namely, the instructions of God through him: Change yourself before fate, your fate, breaks in over you. – And if you did not accept the instructions, you had to or will have to bear it.

And now you say: "I, poor me, am sick because of the other one. I am suffering because of the other one."

What are you doing? You intensify your illness; you intensify your suffering, and then you call: "Lord, Lord, help!" just as the eternal One revealed it. How can the redeeming power, God, your Father, through Me, the Christ, help and stand by you when in the end, you attribute to the other one, that is, to your neighbor, what you have caused yourself and at the same time intensify what you bear?

My children, the ignorance is great on this earth, in this world. Oh see, the world cannot be changed toward the positive from without. The world needs people who actualize the law of love and gradually attain their way out of the law of sowing and reaping. They are then the instruments of selfless love, who do not proselytize in the world, but radiate the law of love. They present it, but do not force anyone to accept what has been actualized by those who pass it on.

God calls you through Me, the Christ. Change yourself! Transform the causal energies up into the positive life forces; this is possible through Me, the Christ in you. The Redeemer-spark absorbs the negative energy, transforms it into positive energy of life – and, in this way, you grow into the spiritual, pure Being.

Oh see, when you accept illness, hardship, fate and the like in the awareness: "I have caused it. Lord, I place it in the divine flame and affirm the positive life forces in me and also in my neighbor. I make an effort to forgive and to ask for forgiveness and to sin no more." – what happens? Your suffering decreases; your illness withdraws, and if you must bear it, because the causal potential is very large, then you sense Me, the bearer of the cross, Christ, in you.

My child, do not look upon the negative! In everything that is negative, find the positive and communicate with it. Affirm the positive in your neighbor, address it and be glad about it. At the same moment, the negative aspects no longer have any power over you.

Dedicate your earthly life to the eternal Father, and you will feel the consecration of your soul, for it is received into the life of God through Me, the Christ. And remember: In suffering is the strength for joy, in illness, health, in unhappiness, happiness, in hatred and animosity, the selfless love. Pay attention to this, and you will no longer say "the other one" – my neighbor, my brother, my sister.

My children, and it will become brighter on this earth through Me, the Christ, and the divine Wisdom. And the world of Christ will develop and the people will be wise. Are you the heralds for this light-filled time? Do you, you, you want to be a herald? Then follow what I have called upon you to do: Love your neighbor as the Father and I, your Redeemer, love you. Do not worry. Plan well and carry out the plan with the divine Wisdom and Love, and you will become stronger in yourself. The inner strength is the power of the Father, who then leads you into the world and puts you to work for Him where it is good for the great totality.

    The spiritual spring is dawning on this earth, even when chaos, war, illness and need still mark the world. The spiritual spring is the Christ with the divine Wisdom. Are you a messenger of the spiritual spring? Yes, are you selfless, are you filled with the power of love? Examine your feelings, thoughts, words and actions. And if you want to become a messenger of the spiritual spring, then go within to the heart of God. The instructions are on the path: Put order in your life. Recognize the will of God. Be wise, earnest, patient, loving and merciful. And if you walk righteously, you are a messenger of the spiritual spring.

    My children, My brothers and sisters, the love of the Father in Me, the Christ, is unending, and I give this love to you very consciously to take with you on your path. The Father loves you. I love you. And this love is the power and the source of strength in each one of you. Go forth, and feel yourselves as blessed ones. Go forth, and actualize, because the spiritual spring is coming. Where do you stand? Where do you stand? Where do all of you stand? At My right hand? I affirm it.

    Go forth in this awareness. I Am with you, for I Am in the Father and the Father in Me, streaming life, from eternity to eternity.

Are You True Christians in My Following?

Christ Revelation, 1990

Verily, I say to you, I Am **the** *Christ. There are many Christs on this earth and in this world, but these Christs are not* **the** *Christ, the Redeemer of all souls and men.*

Recognize and grasp in your hearts that you are cosmic beings! The one who has raised himself to the cosmic Being knows the laws of the All, the universe. He will not ask – he knows. For the one who is immersed in love and wisdom lives in the law of God, in the law of the All, and is also a mighty channel of the All, through which the positive powers flow – to all people, to the nature kingdoms, to all the earth.

Awaken to the cosmic being, whom the Eternal beholds, whom the Eternal created, whom He gave the heritage of infinity, so that you no longer have to hear My word through a human mouth, so that you will have then become the word of life, the law, so that you behold and grasp everything in your inner being. For the one who lives in Me, the one who is the law of the All, knows about all things; nothing is foreign to him. He knows the cosmic correlations and knows that this materialistic world can no longer be saved.

I, the Savior, Christ, spoke to the people as Jesus of Nazareth. But the people did not accept Me – yes, many did not recognize Me. The Jews are still waiting for the Messiah today; but the Messiah was among them and they did not recognize Me.

Again and again, you look for powerful figures in imposing, magnificent garments. That is not humility. Humility is modesty and as Jesus of Nazareth I symbolized modesty.
As long as people adorn their outer person with titles and means, with crimson robes and precious gems, they are impoverished in their hearts and far from the eternal humility, the inner love, the eternal Father in Me, the Christ. They are those who talk about Christ, but are not close to Christ. They use My words: "Christ," "Son of God," "Redeemer" – and in the end, they abuse My word.
This is why I lead you within, so that you find your way to the Christ, who I Am – the love, the gentleness and kindness of your inner being. Grasp and recognize that nothing is hidden to the one who has become the inner light; he sees the so-called most mysterious of things, for everything is manifest in God.

Oh recognize that you are cosmic beings, and if you have developed your inner being, you know the laws of the All. You know that the mighty cosmos can be com-

pared to a cosmic body: The Primordial Central Sun is the head; the mighty suns are the organs; the stars are the particles – you would also call them cells.

You speak of the many Milky Ways – they are the mighty energy channels that supply the organs, the suns and stars with energy. The pure Being and the material cosmos are to be seen as a totality, because a part of the pure cosmos is in the material cosmos, in every planet. And so, the great totality is a huge organism that is supplied by the Primordial Central Sun.

The forces of the All are in constant movement – and so is your earth, too, and even you yourselves. Your bodies consist of cells. Each cell has a spirit consciousness, a consciousness and a subconscious. The spirit consciousness is connected to the pure Being; it communicates with the pure cosmic events. The consciousness and subconscious of each cell communicate with the material cosmos, and thus, the following is guaranteed: No matter what a person thinks, how he speaks, how he acts – this goes into the soul, has its effect in the cells and also goes into the material cosmos, into the finer structure – in the purification planes – and if the thought, the life, of the person is pure, noble and good, he communicates with the forces of the pure Being.

Recognize: Everything is registered in the great cosmos, in the mighty cosmic organism. Each hair is recorded there, because each strand of hair is energy. Everything has its special significance. Nothing is in vain; everything is registered. And so, you might say: Where is free will? You have free will. You can decide for the pure, eternal laws, by living and thinking in a noble and good way, in the spirit of the eternal law. Then peace, harmony, love and health will irradiate your being, your person. You can create your own laws, the so-called ego-law, which is against the pure, eternal law. Then you will also reap this. And so, what you have sown will radiate to you. At every moment you can decide for or against God. Each one bears what he has recorded in the mighty All, the universe. Since God is love, wisdom, power and kindness, **this** will be allotted to **the** person who lives in accordance with the eternal cosmic laws.

Many cannot understand this. For many believe that if they are Christians, that is, if they call themselves Christian, then everything would be accomplished in them; or, when they believe in Me and continue to sin, their sins would nevertheless be removed. This is a human point of view, a denominational way of thinking, which resulted in a power structure that wrongfully uses My name in vain and holds the people in captivity.

Oh see, many speak of Me and yet are far from Me. Denominational thinking is not living in a Christian way. Statesmen take My name for their so-called political parties. I ask of those who truly believe in Me: Is this the Christ – or is My name being misused? Do those who name their parties after My name live in a Christian way? Do your church leaders live in a Christian way? If this were so, then this world would not be a dead body, a corpse, then this world would be a blooming oasis in the cosmic Being.

Oh recognize: The signs are truly giving gale and storm warning. The cosmos is moving ever faster. Many planets are streaming toward the Primordial Central Sun – yes, the whole heaven of Order with its subregions is gradually being led towards the Primordial Central Sun. This means that the primordial power is drawing the heaven of Order closer and closer to itself in order to give it increased energy. The effect of this is light and power in the pure Being, in the astral worlds; the effect is action in the souls, on earth it is transformation, and in the human beings it is likewise action. The causes that have been set are coming into effect more quickly.

Oh recognize, the world speaks of peace. I say to you: The one who does not have peace in his heart cannot bring about peace either. Many speak of selfless love, but the one who does not have it in his heart cannot bring selfless love to his neighbor. The one who wishes happiness and health for his neighbor can bring the *gifts of salvation to his neighbor only when he himself is happy and healthy, because everything is communication.*

If a person is unhappy and wishes his neighbor happiness, his neighbor cannot become happy because the eternal light gives to the neighbor through the one who wished him happiness.

When you wish your neighbor health and you are sick yourself, how can the eternal power give your neighbor health through you? Everything is communication. When you are not in communication with the All-power, how can the All-power work through you and give happiness and health to the one to whom you wished this?

So recognize and grasp in your hearts that no physician can help a patient, if he is sick himself. When a patient goes to the doctor and complains about pain in an organ and the doctor also has pain in the same organ, he will never be able to prepare the organ for the radiation of the Eternal. He won't even find the right medication because he himself suffers from a lack of energy.

How can statesmen lead you in My name when they do not know the inner life, when they do not lead a Christian life, but only abuse My name? How can church leaders lead you to the inner light, when they themselves lack inner light?

Oh recognize: For centuries so-called priests and theologians, pastors – no matter what they call them-

selves – have been teaching from the Bible. When they themselves do not live what they read aloud, the word has no power and does not enter the neighbor.

So look into this world: Who has led you? Many were led astray, because My name was and is abused.

*How much longer do you want to live an externalized life? How much longer do you want to live off a corpse that thoroughly has no life left in it? All those who call themselves Christians and have not lived a Christian life, and do not live one now, have made this world into a cadaver. The earth is suffering and man still pretends to be Christian. Verily, I say to you: The one who believes he still has to live off the corpse called "world" is already a corpse himself and will gradually be carried into the pit along with the great corpse called world – including the Bibles that until now have brought little to the people, because those who teach from them have not actualized the life of salvation. They enacted laws in My name that are not in accordance with the laws of the All. They live a life of external dignity and triviality and do not pay honor to the **One** who beheld and created their spiritual bodies. Corpse to corpse – both will fall into the pit.*

*And so, what do you want to do with **the** Christ? Do you want to worship a Christ, a Christ who I Am* *not – or do you want to find your way to the inner light? Then let go of greed, envy, enmity and unkindness! Move your hearts in the inner light and become consciously brothers and sisters in My Spirit! This world can no longer be saved – but out of the depths of the earth, the spiritual planet, a part-planet, radiates forth. This materialistic system will be pushed away more and more, the forces of nature and much more will contribute to this. The earth is shaking itself and shakes off what is not in the cosmic life, what is not law, love and truth.*

And when you hear that much is going on in the cosmos, then think of My words: The cosmic organism is in increased action. Because of this, the wheel of reincarnation is also turning faster. And if the soul is able to incarnate for only a few days, weeks, months or years, in one instant, it can get rid of much, if it wants to. And so, souls and people are given the chance to discard in a short time the human aspects in them, their sinfulness, so that the soul is better off in the spheres of purification.

Recognize the grace of the Almighty, but recognize the signs of the times, as well. Happy the one who does not bind himself to the corpse world, so that he is not poisoned, for the smell of the corpse is very unpleasant and can lead many a one astray if he is not alert.

Therefore, watch and pray, so that you do not fall into temptation! In many a one of you the soul is strong, but the flesh still limps far behind; it is still weak, and the one who is against Me shows the lusts of the flesh to the flesh.

Recognize and grasp the mighty time in your hearts! The darkness will withdraw – the light comes to this earth. However, before the earth is irradiated with light and power, many a person will have to endure and suffer still much. And if you set out to become the eternal law, you will grow in wisdom and strength, and you will know about the inner life yourselves. For the one who has found the truth knows about all things. He knows the cosmic processes. He knows about communication and thus, enters the cosmic cycle of inner life and is consciously secure in Me. Only the one who does not live in Me worries about tomorrow and is afraid of the future. The one who is truly Christian knows he is secure in Me.

And so, go forth and take My question with you: Are you truly Christian? If yes, then you also live consciously in Me. And if you have doubts about your life as a Christian, examine your feelings, thoughts, words and actions, and you will very gradually experience the human aspects that you have recorded in the cosmos and in your soul. If you earnestly strive to get rid of your human aspects by forgiving, by asking for forgiveness, by making amends; and if you no longer sin, or do the same and like things anymore, you will attain salvation and you will be secure in Me.

When the storms roar over the earth and you are afraid, ask yourself the question: What is not cleared up? Are you still living off the corpse – or do you live in Me, the Christ? Through the movements of the cosmos, you will be led very quickly to your human ego, and the one who discards it will achieve peace, joy, happiness, selfless love and health. And then the soul will breathe the light of the All and every cell will be filled with strength, love and wisdom.

So go forth and examine your life, your thinking and acting – and decide freely. Remember that God is the eternal All, and the All is fine-material life. Everything will be raised to the pure Being, to the fine-material life again, for the Fall is coming to an end in the cycle of eons. Do you want to suffer or to live in inner joy? Do you want to enjoy outer love or to live in selfless love? However you decide, I leave it up to you. Go forth, and examine your life. Are you true Christians in My following? Go forth, and think over your way of living and thinking.

I Am **the** Christ, not **any** Christ – I Am the life in each one of you. You do not need to go here and there *in order to take up communication with Me. Go into your inner being! In your inner being burns the light of redemption – this Am I! Go, and become the cosmic peace and you will be true loving ones.*

My blessing and My strength flow to you in peace.

Peace.

Do You Want to Be My Disciple?

Christ Revelation, 1998

With the greeting of the heavens, I step into your midst with My spirit body.*
Peace be with you.

Feel into your hearts; feel the Christ in you, who is present among you with His spirit body, so that you may recognize how close I Am to you. Do you recognize Me in your hearts? Then you have found Me and have found your way to your selves, to your true Being. If you do not recognize Me in your hearts, you have not found your way to your true Being and still feel like strangers to the eternal Being, yet like natives of this world.

My kingdom is not of this world. My kingdom is a kingdom of the Spirit and a kingdom of peace. Happy the one who recognizes Me. He has attained victory over the flesh.

Oh see, 2000 years ago, after My resurrection I stepped among My apostles and some of My disciples

---

**This revelation was not only given from the stream of the omnipresent Spirit of the Christ of God, but Christ was also present as spirit being, that is, in the spirit body.*

with the greeting: Peace be with you. The apostles were frightened, fearful and could not believe it. They thought a so-called spirit was among them. Two thousand years have gone by. Where does so-called Christianity stand? Have the Christians taken Me in? If yes, then I Am resurrected in them; then they recognize Me and their joy is great, because they feel that they have become one with Me.

Whoever has found Me recognizes Me in his neighbor, for I, the Christ of God, meet you in many different shapes and forms. "Peace be with you," shines from the eyes of your fellowman. Do you feel the greeting of peace in your hearts when you meet your neighbor? Or do you look only at the faults of your fellowman? Then you have not yet recognized Me.

Oh see: The eternal One sacrificed divine beings and sacrifices them again and again. They came down and took on flesh. They were and are the prophets and enlightened men and women. The eternal One also sacrificed the Co-Regent of the heavens. I went to the earth and became a human being. I brought the glad tidings of the inner life to mankind and taught the people the way into the Father's house. I brought the God of love and mercy to the people and showed them the path to life via the commandments.

Oh see: It is a plain and simple path; it is the path of mercy. How did and do the people act toward the proph-

ets, the enlightened men and women? How did they act toward Me, Jesus of Nazareth? First "Hosanna!" then "Crucify Him!"

Many a one believes that God, My eternal Father, who is also your Father, sacrificed Me through people for people. God is not an avenging God. God is not a God of death, but God is the life. He sacrificed and sacrifices divine beings, who go into the flesh, into the earthly garment, in order to announce and proclaim the glad tidings of life. But the people, the sinners, who did not want to accept the bread of life, are the ones who slaughtered Me. And so, I hung on the beam of death, tortured and slaughtered by sinners, who were afraid of the glad tidings, for they proclaimed another message that was and is binding.

Many prophets were slaughtered, mistreated, tortured, mocked and scorned. Why? Because the folk, the people, remained sinners and felt comfortable in the hotbed of sin. It was not God, the great love and mercy, who sacrificed His children by way of people. He sent them to the people in order to bring the message of love and of mercy. This was and is the sacrifice from the divine Being, the sacrifice of God.

God, Himself, the mighty Creator-power, sacrificed and sacrifices Himself daily in the nature kingdoms. But how did man behave and how does he behave today? After 2000 years, the animals are still hanging from the beams in the slaughterhouses, like I did as Jesus of Nazareth. After 2000 years, the bodies of the animals are torn open, hacked up and prepared for the palates of the so-called Christians. Do you not know that you cannot live without your divine heritage, to which the nature kingdoms also belong? Do you not know that man and nature should form a unity? Just as the spirit beings form a unity in heaven with infinity, with pure nature, so should human beings become unity and form unity.

But what is going on after 2000 years? People continue to be tortured. People continue to be discriminated against; those sent by God are ridiculed and the animals are hung on beams in slaughterhouses.

Oh see: What you do to the least of My brothers you are doing to Me. And what you do to the nature kingdoms you are doing to the mighty Creator-Spirit. And so, what you do to people and to the nature kingdoms, you do, in turn, to yourselves, because everything in all things is your divine heritage; it is the essence of life, and life is unity.

Oh see: you look your fellowman in the eye. What do you think? How do you talk about your neighbor? Do you not know that through your negativity you entangle yourselves more and more and create your fate? Is what mankind had and has to bear still not enough? Where do the illnesses, the miseries, the worries, the poverty and much more come from? From heaven or from you? You create them yourselves, because you do not want to develop your divine heritage and thus, you do not recognize yourselves. How do you want to recognize Me?

The misery is great on this earth, in this world. But the misery is each one, himself, and in the causal entanglement, it is all people together. It is a great network that draws over the earth and each one of you has created many of these knots or is tied to the so-called knots. And this network is, in turn, in the spheres of purification and in the material cosmos.

Oh see, and feel in your hearts: In the end, all your unlawfulness is directed against you. Animals are tormented, people disdained, animals hung from beams in slaughterhouses, cut into pieces, animals deliberately tread upon. And if you look into your plant world – which plant is still as it was, originally? Man has changed and crossbred everything; he invaded nature, changed and tormented it, right up until this hour. Do you not know that all this vibrates in the so-called causal network, to which you are connected according to your way of feeling, thinking, speaking and wanting?

Oh see: This mighty Creator-Spirit sacrifices itself; the trees, the bushes bear fruit. But are you satisfied with this? Only the fewest are satisfied with what the great garden gives them; they want ever more, ever more – why? Because mankind has turned away more and more from the Christ of God, who I Am, that is, it has shadowed itself and still does, and thus man is poor in light and strength. So he grabs, looks for more and more, and thus, meat and the carnal must be, for food and for the body.

Oh see: I meet you in many shapes. I meet you in your fellowman. I greet you, even when the person speaks differently – in every person is the greeting of peace, "Peace be with you." A gentle breath goes through the person. Is he received by you, by your hearts, in the awareness that, yes, I am meeting a person, but in the person I am meeting Christ? Only when you understand that I encounter you in your fellowman, only when you comprehend that the great, mighty Creator-Spirit meets you in every little animal, in every plant, in every stone, will you recognize Me, because step by step, you are doing the will of the Eternal, which is also My will.

Oh see: With every talk against your fellowman, you turn away from Me. With everything that you do, also by your compulsive actions, whereby your neighbor should and must do what you want, you turn away from Me. But many pray and pray; many of you have prayed today. I ask you: Could God, your Father and Mine, receive your prayers? Do you do what you pray for? How often do you ask for mercy for yourselves?

You seek compassion and call upon the kind God for compassion and mercy. Are you merciful toward your fellowman? Are you merciful toward nature, toward each and every creature? Are you merciful?

Oh see: If you had developed a tiny spark of love for God, as large as a mustard seed, then you would sense what mercy means: compassion, sympathy for your fellowman, compassion for the animals, which likewise feel and sense, compassion for all plants, for the mineral world. Then you would treat carefully the great gifts of creation, the sacrificial offerings of nature, for God sacrifices Himself daily for His human children.

Oh see: Again and again you hear the great mystery of life, the word, which I Am, through the mouth of a prophet. How many words have you already heard? Do you not know that I place your whole heritage, the essence of infinity, into every word through the mouth of a prophet? How much of this have you grasped? How much of this have you put into practice?

Oh see: If you would sense the meaning of the words through the mouth of a prophet, then you would be as though transformed; then you would recognize Me, because you have recognized yourselves as conscious sons and daughters of God. But how often have I been crucified by you, crucified, over and over again? You sin despite knowing better and believe you are too weak to accept your life, the true Being. The one who wants to, can do it; the one who does not want to, speaks of weakness. But the one who loves – only as much as a grain of sand or a mustard seed – feels what I mean by love and mercy, for he feels Me in his heart and senses My physical presence.

Verily, I seek you; I seek you; I seek you! Do you want to be My disciple? Then follow Me! Do what I taught you as Jesus of Nazareth and what I teach you as Christ. Follow Me, and you will experience the risen One in you, because you will have overcome death and will find yourself in the life that is your divine heritage.

Many a one wanders for hundreds, thousands, of years. They speak about the truth – and do not know it. They say nice words – and remain unspiritual. Verily, many a one of you made the covenant with the Eternal in the so-called Old Testament, broke it and made it again in the New Covenant with God, and many a one broke it again. The covenant broken two times, journey upon journey, until you have found the neighbor whom you have left lying on the road to life, because you were too preoccupied with yourself and favored certain people. Do you not know that when you favor one person, you disregard, that is, neglect Me?

You say that it is difficult to achieve peace and unity with all people. You, O man, begin with yourself. What *you favor is always your disadvantage. And if you become free from your value judgments, your preferences, you will become steadfast and stable in Me and will be **the** disciple who truly follows Me. Then you will be kind, loving and gentle, because you have attained understanding and out of the understanding, empathy. The one who beholds his neighbor, beholds Me. The one who beholds the nature kingdoms senses the mighty Creator-Spirit and very gradually feels what unity means.*

Oh see: All the formulas of your church institutions – no matter how you call them – are of no use to you. Again and again priests appeared and made the people believe they could lead them to God. Where do your priests of today stand, your pastors, your so-called church leaders? Before their own word – and it is a dead word, because it has no spiritual content, but only form and beyond the form, only binding. What have your church leaders brought you? Every year the same rituals, every year the same formulas and last but not least, the same prayers. The one who trusts them will one day mourn over himself, because he entrusted himself to people instead of building on the Spirit, who dwells in him.

Verily, verily, I say to you: The hour has long since come, in which you should have recognized who dwells in you. My disciples, yes, you are the temple of the

One Spirit. Sanctify this, by doing the will of God; then you will recognize Me; then you will be merciful, because you are loving; then you will be kind, because you have learned to understand.

You, My brother, you, My sister, I call you: Do you want to follow Me? Do you want to be My disciple? For I have come into your midst physically in corporal form – with you, with you, I want to establish the Kingdom of Peace. But may one thing be said to you: Do not bind yourself to any person. Make peace with your fellowman, and keep peace. And find yourself again and again in the center, which I Am, and you will establish the inner kingdom with your brothers and sisters. For it is needed. The world is burning. The Spirit rises out of the fire. Will you be there? I Am calling you!

Verily, verily, My disciples keep peace among each other. They are peaceful toward everyone and everything. But they do not follow the carnal desires of their neighbor. They are in the center, and I Am the center.
Oh see: I want to resurrect in you, so that you recognize Me and with My power overcome your still existing sinfulness, so that you may become spirit of My Spirit, torches of love and mercy. And many a one will say: "Who can know God? Who can know even Christ? We are human beings!" I make a difference

between knowing and recognizing. And if you do this, you can recognize Me in many aspects of life and if one recognition follows another, you will find Me, because you will have found yourself as a son or daughter of God and, after this earthly existence, you will stand before Me and know Me, because I Am your brother. Will you know God, the Eternal? You will know the Father, the corporal form. There is no word to express what it means when you behold your Father and know Him. But you will never know the primordial power, the eternally pulsating Creator-power, the eternal power of evolution. This is the streaming, eternally creative, giving Spirit, which respirates infinity and creates ever more forms and heavenly worlds, where the beings of love live and have their eternal home.

*Come – come and follow Me! Be **with** your neighbor, be **for** your neighbor, but do not bind yourself to him. Demand nothing of him that you can do yourself. Then you will develop the strength in the Spirit, and I Am this strength in you.*

The mighty Creator-power gives itself untiringly. It sacrifices itself. You will partake of the meal – it is a sacrifice of the Creator-power out of love for you. For this reason, you should partake of every meal consciously, in the awareness that the mighty Creator-power has given itself to you. It gives itself untiringly.

Accept the gifts consciously, and you will recognize Me, because you will have found yourselves as the Self, which I Am.

Oh know, and sense in your hearts: I remain among you in corporal form, the Christ who blesses, who calls disciples who follow Him consciously, since He wants to establish the inner kingdom, the Kingdom of Peace, with them. It will be small and inconspicuous, and it will become great, when you grow in My Spirit.

So remain in Me and know that I remain among you. My Spirit is in you, eternally. And if you are again spirit of My Spirit, you are also again spirit from the Primordial Spirit and are one with the Father and with Me.

I spread My hands, My arms, out over you in blessing, and I remain among you in corporal form, giving peace, giving love and giving mercy.

Peace.

Feel ME Present in You

God-Father Revelation, 1990

Thus speaks your Lord and God, your eternal Father.

My children, you have gathered in My Spirit and in the Spirit of My Son and you have opened your hearts in prayer for the one Spirit of love, who I Am – who I Am in the Son, who I Am in you.

Children of My heart, think of the mighty time. Feel that I, your Father, through Christ, your brother and Redeemer, draw ever closer to you. Feel that you are not alone.

For many of you it is hard to change your way of thinking, yes, to turn back and to renounce your human aspects. Children, see: You have to feel Me more, so that it is easier for you to renounce your human aspects and to align yourself with your true being, with the inner life that you are in compressed form.

It is written that you should make no image of Me, for I Am the impersonal power, the light, the love, the stream, the salvation, the eternal law. See, the primordial power is the omnipresent power that flows through all things. Whether you call the primordial *power the eternal law, the eternal love, eternal peace or All-power, or Being, it is the impersonal life that flows. It is My breath, which is omnipresent.*

Since I gave you form from the All-power, the eternal law, the impersonal life, I also gave Myself form. And thus, I Am your Father, and, like you, the All that has taken on form. Just as you go through the heavenly planes in all spheres of the eternal Being, so do I, too, go through the heavenly planes in all spheres, as the All that has taken on form – the Father in the All-stream, in the law, in My breath. Just as I move through the All, so you, too, move through the All, once you are pure beings again.

This is how I see you. And this is also how I see you in movement. Children, recognize that you are absolute, independent beings. This is the freedom. You are absolutely independent, because I have given you everything as essence and power that I, as the All that has taken on form, as the Father, bear within Me.

As a being, I, your Father, Am the All that has taken on form. You, My children, as beings are the All that has taken on form. All the powers of infinity are in you – and you are these powers yourselves as the All that has taken on form, just as I, as your Father.

You are absolutely free, because you are independent, since you have everything that I have. I have kept nothing back, nothing for Me. What I have as the All that has taken on form, you, the All that has taken on form, also have. The stream, the eternal power, the law, is the all-maintaining life; it is the primordial power, which I Am, as the impersonal Being.

But I, too, your Father, move as you move yourselves, as independent beings in the primordial stream, in the eternal law, which holds all the heavenly bodies together, which forms the pathways of the All – so that you can move around, so that you can be free, so that you can live selflessly and independently. But everything that flows is compressed Being in you; this is our All-body.

Children, feel, finally, what I want to say to you with this. I Am not the distant God, the mighty, wrathful, avenging God, who sends you to damnation, who chastises and punishes you. Children, oh, no! Oh, no! Now, in these earthly moments, I say: Children, oh, no!

I love you and this love becomes apparent in the Son, in you and through you.

See: As I feel, so do you feel as pure beings. We feel that which is: freedom, equality, unity, justice, and among yourselves, brotherliness, and I among you as your Father, eternally.

Because you are independent beings, you have the freedom to do what you feel like, in heaven as well as on earth. The beings in heaven do what the All is: freedom, lawfulness, selfless love and peace. They are the law, because they live the All-law, and thus, they also move in the All. In all of infinity there is no point where My own cannot be, because My power is in every tiny point, which they, in turn, bear in themselves. Because of this, they can be everywhere, because everything is in them. This is also in you.

Independence is also given to you as human beings. It is the free will. You can decide freely at every moment. You decide in your feelings and thoughts, with your words and actions.

See, when you say: "I want to live without worry or care," then this is a thought, an input, an entry into the All-law. Now it depends on what you make of this input in the All-law. All your brothers and sisters in the eternal Being live without worry. They know no worry, because they live in the All-law, in the fullness, and consciously bear everything within themselves and not only preserve it, but also fulfill it.

When you now say: "I want to live without worry," then you must leave your neighbor his freedom and cause him no worry, be it in sensations, thoughts, words or deeds. At the moment you cause your neighbor to worry, you reverse the first thought: "I want to live without worry." You reverse it and make it negative because you cause your neighbor to worry. At the same time, you can be sure that what you think or say toward your neighbor will cause you worry.

See, children, this is the free will. But when you introduce into the All-law: "I want to live without worry," then, at the same time, you have to nurture the corresponding feelings, thoughts, words and actions – then you will indeed live without worry or care, because then I, your Father, take care of you.

You will then also take care of your neighbor, by being for him and with him, in your feelings, thoughts, words and deeds. This is how the community of the children of God develops. And in this way, you will grow into the law of love, which is your heritage.

Children, recognize that you are selfless beings – and at the same time, independent. What you enter into the mighty eternal All, as beings of light, is what you establish communication with. This comes back to you – again strength, light, beauty, purity, perfection, the law of peace. The same is true in reverse. What you think comes back to you.

And if you say: "I want peace in my soul, peace in my surroundings. I want harmony and love," then you enter this into the All-law. If you live accordingly in your feelings, thoughts, words and actions – toward your fellowman, toward the plant, animal and mineral worlds – then you have immediate communication with the eternal All-law, which is your true being, which you are, yourself: compressed power of the All.

Children! Is it so hard for you to change your way of thinking – if you are aware that you are selfless beings? You are the All that has taken on form. You are independent beings. As selfless, independent beings, you can move everywhere and you are protected by the power, love and wisdom, by Me, through Christ.

Children! It is written: You shall make no image of Me. But I now give you a picture, so that you can recognize yourself in this picture and move in it:
Do not see the earth as just a dark place where sin prevails. See a picture in which everything is light. With the help of this picture, transform the earth and your surroundings, and not lastly, yourself, into light and power. Wherever you go, draw the picture: You walk on streets of light.
When you meet people, no matter of what attitude or outlook, put into the picture that they are infinitely loved by Me, that deep in their soul they are radiant beings, your brothers and sisters, whom you do not know externally, but who live in you, in your inner being. You know them because you know yourselves. And so, suddenly you see radiant beings.
No matter what you do, say: "The power of the Lord is in my hands. Whatever I touch is life; it is the power of the Lord. Whatever I do, I do with the power of the Lord." And then see everything that you do as radiating light.

When you go here and there and meet animals, plants and stones, say: "The power of the Lord is in each of them." See the animal, plant and mineral worlds as light and power. See how joy, peace and harmony radiate from them.

When you go to your earthly families or move among your earthly families and relatives, say: "They are all my brothers and sisters." Your earthly brothers, your earthly sisters are loved by Me and are brothers and sisters in the light of love.

When you say: "This is my husband. This is my wife. These are my children" – see them as brothers and sisters and as a part of you. Should the shell – for example, the shell of your earthly brother, the shell of your earthly sister – leave you, carry them in your heart, despite everything. No matter how the shell acts, carry the innermost being in your heart, and you can be sure you will have to endure neither need nor worry. I, your Father, will take care of you! The prerequisite is: Do not quarrel with your neighbor. Do not cling to him or her, by binding him or her to you with all possible arguments. Trust, my child, I Am here!

And in this way, you will all transform the earth into light and power, because you have this picture of the earth. No matter where you go, you see purity and beauty in the picture, even when the external world shows other forces. And now, how do you see yourself in this picture? How do you move in this picture?

You should make no image of Me. But make yourselves the following picture: I, the All-power, move in you. I radiate through you as light and power. And so, see your body as a body of light and power, which is permeated with beauty, purity, with the noble and fine.

How do you then move in this picture? How do you think and feel in this transformed picture? Ever more divinely! In this way, you feel Me, your Father, present in you, through you. And you will make no image of Me for yourselves. If you have attained the gift to truly feel yourselves as radiant beings, with pure, noble feelings, thoughts, words and actions, with fine features on your countenance, in your movements and the like, then you will no longer speak of age, but of inner youth.

And just as you then see yourselves, you will recognize yourselves as the images of God and you will sense that just as you radiate, so do I, your Father, radiate.

See, what I have as the Father, you, too, have as selfless, independent beings – just as I Am selfless and independent, your Father.

I Am your Father, because I have given you everything. You are the All that has taken on form. What streams is the primordial power, the life, in which you move. It is the omnipresent stream, which goes forth from the primordial law and will be eternally. So was and is the primordial law – eternally. It is the forces of the All, which are eternal. Out of them, I gave Myself the form. Out of them, I gave you form.

Children, what more do you want?

Do you now know, you foolish human children, what you have to do? Discard this foolishness and feel what you are.

And come closer to Me, your Father, with the power of the Son, with the Redeemer-power – and you will feel what it means to be children of the Eternal. Children of the Eternal means to again be children in the eternal All-stream. For the Eternal, who I Am in the All-stream, simply is the All-power, the omnipresent Being, the life in you. If the All-power were not omnipresent, you could not live. This **is** the breath; this **is** the life, which also permeates Me, the form, the being.

Children! Draw this picture of light over your feelings, thoughts, words and actions. Then you will transform yourselves, and through you, the earth will very gradually restructure itself. It will become more and more light-filled, brighter. It will vibrate higher, because you are light and power and you live in Me consciously, yes, you vibrate in Me.
Children, My word flows through My instrument, through your sister. But grasp the depth in the word,

*and you will feel My love. And this love **is**, and will never pass away, just as you are, and will never pass away, because you are children of the All, My children.*

*Now little child, discard your foolish person. Be! Be! Then you will hear the Being knocking in you, which I Am, which ultimately you are, too. And you will feel that we are united, from eternity to eternity, immortal, because the eternal law and the eternal homeland are immortal, since the eternal principle simply is eternal. And this is how we **are**. And this is how we remain. And this is how you will be once again – totally consciously, eternally.*

And we, from eternity to eternity.

God Breathes Back the Fall. The True Life Opens Up

Christ Revelation, 1993

Peace be with you.

With this heavenly greeting, I, Christ, step into your midst. In this hour, which has been sanctified by God, our Father, I speak to you as your brother.

My beloved brothers and sisters, the Kingdom of God is the kingdom of infinite love. Thus, my kingdom is not of this world. My kingdom is a kingdom of the Spirit, a kingdom of infinite love. And this unending kingdom of eternal love will come to this earth. For this reason, rejoice, all you faithful ones, all you righteous ones! For the earth is cleansing itself and the Kingdom of Peace, the kingdom of infinite love, is coming onto this earth that is cleansing itself more and more.

In this hour, which has been sanctified by God, our eternal Father, I call all faithful ones to deep and holy prayer. You will ask: Who are the faithful? They are all those men and women, brothers and sisters, who day after day clear up their sinful aspects, no longer do them, and thus, step by step, they fulfill the laws of the Kingdom of God. I call them to a deep and holy prayer.

Come, beloved brothers and sisters. Go with Me, your brother, into the kingdom of the inner being. Yes, I guide your senses to within, so that you may feel that I Am your brother, and that the Kingdom of God must be opened up in the inner being, so that it can become externally visible in this world.

Raise your senses to the Eternal One, and pray with Me, your brother.
Eternal, infinite Father,
holy, holy, holy are You,
great All-One.
Your infinite love, wisdom, greatness and justice stream through infinity and seize all those who raise their hearts to You.
Eternal, infinite beloved One, we thank you with all our hearts, with all the forces of infinity, by fulfilling what is our own: the holy, eternal law of infinite, selfless love.
Great, mighty Father, as a stream, You are the Father-Mother-God and You set all of Your children aglow. We are fulfilled and set aglow by Your holy will, Your holy law, which is our being, our heritage, yes, which we are, ourselves, as beings that have taken on form.

Infinitely eternal One, infinitely eternal Being, the glory of the heavens comes to this earth through all righteous men and women, brothers and sisters. Holy One, holy One, holy One, You just, loving Father, all of creation bows before You, all beings of the Being and all righteous brothers and sisters. Heaven rejoices and the beings jubilate in inner joy, because the angel before the throne of love soars through all realms and through all spheres of purification, calling again and ever again: It is done! It is done!

Glorious One, it is done only because You are the glory in us, the infinite love, which encompasses all children, which bears everyone in its heart. Kind All-One, infinitely eternal Being, we bow down before You, before Your greatness and glory – Father, Father in us, and we in You, as Your children.

Beloved brothers and sisters, verily, I come to you as your brother. You heard in the prayer: It is done. In the words "It is done," is also contained: It is over. It is over for the Fall, because the Eternal One is breathing back the Fall. It is over for ever returning incarnations, to burden oneself anew. It is over for the eras, during which the Fall lasted.

Yes, God, the Eternal, God, our eternal Father, is breathing back the Fall. For all people this means that this materialistic world is passing away, that very gra-

dually the time of probation is receding and this earth will become a place of expiation. Yes, this is taking place very gradually, for in the eternally streaming Being there is nothing static; it is a gradual reversal. The time of probation is receding; expiation is coming to the fore more and more. This means that whoever is in the process of expiation can no longer sin.

The one who is still on probation may still sin; but the following applies to those people who are on probation: Recognize and clear up, **before** *your sin becomes effective. And so, in probation lies the unending grace and help to recognize and clear up the sins in time. And the one who no longer commits them fulfills the eternal laws of love step by step, thus maturing into the divine, into the eternal life.*

Expiation means that there is no longer any probation. The sins become effective and assault the soul – and the body, as long as the soul is still in the earthly garment.

Oh recognize that it will be on earth as it is in the spheres of purification. In the spheres of purification, there is no probation, but immediate expiation, that is, the sin becomes effective and the soul experiences this on its soul body. This is also what is taking place on this earth, to wit, very, very gradually.

And so, the time of probation withdraws from the one who listens to the laws of life for a long time and hardly actualizes them, and he enters into expiation. In this way, the earth also purifies itself more quickly.

Oh recognize the countless plagues and illnesses in this world, the miseries and worries; the world is rebelling and you are experiencing this more and more. In this, you recognize that this world is entering expiation and with it all people who hear the word of salvation and do not do it. And all those who hear the word and also talk about it, that is, talk about the laws of life and do not do them, have not yet consciously accepted the filiation to God. They call themselves the masters of this world. They call themselves authorities, give themselves titles and sit in prominent places.

Oh, see! They all have to become children of God, for in the law of infinite love is equality, freedom, unity, brotherliness and justice. Unity means that in the Spirit of the Lord all are brothers and sisters, of one spirit. And this unity bears freedom in itself. And freedom makes you strong, and in this strength is justice. And the one who is just fulfills more and more the law of infinite love.

My beloved brothers and sisters, this is why the following may be said to you: Equip yourselves to actualize; this means, to still make use of the time of probation, for it is receding from you. But all those, *who are called and open their hearts and now begin to recognize the laws of love, to accept them and to actualize them every day, still live in this opportunity of probation. When it withdraws totally from the earth, then it is expiation. And expiation means chaos, so to speak. No matter where you look – chaos.*

Oh see, also in this way, this materialistic world is coming to an end, because the Eternal One is breathing back the Fall. He breathes it back from the earth. In the spheres of purification, expiation will continue to take place.

The angel calls: It is done! It is done! It is done! It is over! It is over! It is over! All true prophets, all righteous men and women will be vindicated. Everything that was done to justice, love and wisdom must be atoned for. And in the word "over," the image can be seen: The ropes are laid out – Satan will be fettered. It is over with all that he did – also in My name. It is over; the ropes are drawing ever tighter. They are pulled taut very slowly. And the one who is caught in these ropes is the one who does not want to let the Kingdom of God, the infinite selfless love, come to the earth.

And so, you, My beloved brothers and sisters, are experiencing a great time, and all those who are prepared in their hearts to receive the inner life more and more – yes, they rejoice and jubilate in the inner joy with the pure beings and bow before the All-One in deep, holy prayer.

Oh see, the true life is opening up. The life in peace, in freedom and in unity, and thus, in brotherliness. Then there will be no authorities and no subordinates anymore. All people who have accepted in their hearts the filiation to God will then be brothers and sisters and worship the One who is their, our, Father. And then, on this earth that is cleansing itself more and more, people will live who are united in the brotherhood of Christ, that is, with Me, and I Am consciously their friend and their brother and, at the same time, the ruler of the Kingdom of God on this earth. And it will be glorious. Yes, the glory of the eternal Father will be among the righteous brothers and sisters, and there will be no duplicity on this hallowed land anymore.

Yes, verily I say to you that I Am now preparing this inner life. How? By calling you to fulfill the laws of infinite love more and more, so that I can work **through you**. I am not coming to build a city. I come through all righteous men and women, brothers and sisters, to establish the inner kingdom, the Kingdom of Peace, the kingdom of infinite, eternal love. And so, the earth is already preparing itself from within. Just as the eternal Jerusalem radiates onto the earth, so does the spiritual part-planet radiate to the surface of the earth, linking with the holy radiation of the eternal Primordial Father.

Holy, holy, holy are You, O Eternal One, who sends the rays and through Me calls all those who have opened their hearts for You and live the filiation deep in their hearts. They are the builders of the Kingdom of God and the inhabitants of the Kingdom of Peace of Jesus Christ.

And there will be no duplicity on this land anymore. Rejoice! The moons are dwindling away – you say: "The times are dwindling away." And it will be. Yes, what the prophets of the Old Covenant announced is very gradually beginning: the Kingdom of God on this earth that is cleansing itself. There will be places on the earth where it is still dark, for you know that Satan will be bound. After moons – you would say: after times – he will be allowed to measure himself once more on the inner kingdom and on this earth. But his fight will be of short duration, because the earth is becoming ever finer, ever more light-filled; what is coarse-material and dense will blast away from it, and the pure part-planet will rise more and more in order to very gradually reintegrate into the primordial stream.

Moons, moons – you talk about times, times – but what are times in eternity, in the great love of our eternal Father? Do not think of times. Think of eternity – it is love. And this infinite, eternal love radiates to *you through Me, Christ. And this infinite love of the Father-Mother-God wants to touch you more and more and guide you out of the chaos of this world, to the inner kingdom; for when the inner kingdom opens up in each one of you, then it will come to this earth, through you – yes, through you! Remember that you are in the flesh now – so it is through you; yes, you could do great things if I could be effective through you.*

Let yourselves be touched by the infinite, eternal love, and be seized by the eternal Father, who loves all of you. O brother, O sister, do not say you are a sinner. See: God, your eternal Father, the Father of us all, beholds you in His heart as the beloved, pure child, which He beheld and created. And He radiates this infinite love to you. Feel the radiation and you will recognize your sins, clear them up and no longer do them. In your innermost being, be sure that God loves you, even if you are still a sinner.

And the one who recognizes his sins each day, who clears them up and no longer does them and fulfills the laws of salvation step by step will not live in want; for everything is prepared for the faithful ones who live in the awareness of the Father's love. They will neither live in want nor starve. They will have everything that they need as human beings, because they are children of love, and the children of love live in the divine fullness.

Verily, verily, I say to you: All is done and thus, also prepared for those who have opened their hearts and live in the awareness of the filiation to God.

*The Fall developed because one being, and then more beings, did not want to accept and receive the filiation to God. But the person who has received it **now**, yes, who bears it in his heart, is a brother, a sister, a child, and thus, a son or a daughter of the infinite love and may now say: "I am in the Father and the Father is in me. We are one." This is how I spoke as Jesus of Nazareth: The Father and I are one. And this is also how you should speak, you who live in the filiation to God, yes, who fulfill it day after day: "The Father and I are one." – And so, we, too, are consciously one in the brotherhood and sisterhood, because we – you and I – are brothers and sisters, sons and daughters of the infinite, eternal love.*

*Oh recognize, you have come together for the supper at the table of the Lord, an inner meal. **How** did you come? Did you come in brotherhood, as brothers, as sisters? Or do you imagine yourself to be something better? Then hurry, before the time of probation is totally taken away. And if you have truly come to the table of the Lord as brothers, as sisters, then you feel one with each other and one with Me, your brother, Christ. And the one who feels one with his neighbor* feels as one with Me and is consciously in the Father and the Spirit of the Father is consciously in him. He then lives in the aliveness of the eternal law, and this is joy, inner, vivifying joy.

My beloved brothers and sisters, are you truly in the brotherhood and sisterhood, then you are in the brotherhood with Me. And I say to you that you will lack nothing. Then I will work through you and establish what comes from the heavens and out of the depths of the earth: the Kingdom of Peace.

The angels of love step into your midst. They are carrying bowls, filled with the water of life. They go to all righteous brothers and sisters and they ask you: Drink. Drink from it, all of you. This water is balm; it is salvation and strength, inner victory and deep joy. Drink, drink the water of life.
They also step before all of you who do not yet feel themselves to be children of love and they ask the question: Brother, sister, do you want to drink? If you now turn back and change your ways, then drink – for the water of life is balm. It gives you power and strength, so that you may clear up what you have recognized as sinful and no longer do, so that you may join the flock of righteous brothers and sisters.
Drink, yes, drink, all who open their hearts for Me, the Christ of God. Drink – and feel the beings of light.

Yes, with Me, they sanctify this hour, so that it goes into eternity to the One who is eternal: holy, holy, holy.

My beloved brothers and sisters, the messengers of God and I, your brother and Redeemer, share the bread of love with you. I go through the rows and the beings of light accompany Me. Yes, I touch each and every one of you and I want to break the bread with each one of you. And the one who consciously breaks it with Me and partakes of it with Me absorbs the essence of life in his soul. And the soul glows more and more with the fullness of love, and the soul will lack nothing and thus, not the human being either.

And so, I go through the rows, and I will take My place at the table of the Eternal One, as His representative. For we – you, the righteous ones, with Me, Christ – are working for the great Spirit, so that the glory can be among you and the Eternal One can sit with you at the table and I, with Him, as your brother.

So I touch you with the heavenly peace. Yes, I immerse it into your hearts. Receive the meal of love.

Peace.

Books in the Universal Life Series

This Is My Word –
A and Ω – The Gospel of Jesus
The Christ Revelation,
which true Christians the world over have come to know

A book that lets you really get to know about Jesus, the Christ, about the truth of his activity and life as Jesus of Nazareth.

From the contents: The falsification of the teachings of Jesus of Nazareth during the past 2000 years - Jesus loved the animals and always spoke up for them - Meaning and purpose of a life on earth - Jesus taught about marriage - God is not a wrathful God - The teaching of "eternal damnation" is a mockery of God - Life after death - Equality between men and women - The coming times and the future of mankind, and much more!

1078 pages / Order No. S 007en, ISBN: 978-1-890841-17-1

NEW!

The Word of the Christ of God –
to Mankind Before this World Passes Away
Nearer to God In You

Believe, trust, hope and endure! What do these mean and how can we apply them on our way to God? How do we turn belief into an active faith? How do we develop trust? Hope is expressed in setting goals that are carried out with confidence. What does it mean to endure in the divine sense? Experience the Inner Path in condensed form. Simple clear words, given to all people who long for God and a fulfilled, happy life in freedom. A gift from God to all His human children.

112 pages / Order No. S 139en, ISBN: 978-1-890841-45-4

God Heals

There is a mighty, indescribable power in us. It is the central power of love, God's power and healing. Learn how this power in you can be unfolded!

61 pages / Order No. S 309en, ISBN: 978-1-890841-23-2

NEW!

The Path to Cosmic Consciousness –
Happiness, Freedom and Peace

The path to cosmic consciousness is the path to inner happiness and inner peace, to the feeling of having "arrived." Where? In the Kingdom of God, of which Jesus, the Christ, already taught, that it can be found within, in every person. It is our true, divine being. This is a path of liberation, which Gabriele, the prophetess and messenger of God, walked ahead of us. As a guide, she showed how we can learn not only to fulfill our work more quickly and conscientiously, but also how we can make peace with our fellowman and with nature and the animals, and how we can maintain it. Through this, we become happy and free!

75 pages / Order No. S 341en, ISBN: 978-1-890841-60-7

The Sermon on the Mount –
Life in Accordance With the Law of God

Timeless instructions for a peaceful and fulfilled life. A path that leads the way out of the dead-end in which so many people find themselves today. An excerpt from a work of revelation "This Is My Word."

112 pages / Order No. S 008en, ISBN: 978-1-890841-42-3

Live the Moment –
and You Will See and Recognize Yourself

Now, in this instant, the state of our soul shows itself. We can see it in our feelings, thoughts, words and actions that take place at every moment in us. Become sensitive to the signals of your inner life...

76 pages / Order No. S 315en, ISBN: 978-1-890841-54-6

Where Did I Come From? Where Am I Going?

The wherefrom and whereto of our life is no longer a mystery. Following explanations on the important questions on life after death, answers are given to 75 most frequently asked questions on this topic.

75 pages / Order No. S 407en, ISBN: 978-1-890841-09-6

NEW!

Cause and Development of All Illness
What a person sows, he will reap

A book more relevant than ever before, more exciting than a thriller, more moving than a documentary ... Many details revealed over 20 years ago by the Spirit of God are confirmed today by science: Without a healthy, balanced relationship between human beings, animals, plants and minerals, mankind will not survive in the long run. What does this mean for the future? What are the effects of man's destructive behavior toward nature, the animals and, not least, his own state of health? Learn about until now unknown correlations and frontier zones between spirit and matter, about the effect of the power of thoughts on our life, for instance, how harmful parasites and pathogens can be created by our behavior patterns, about holistic healing, the meaning of life on earth, and much more ...

360 pages / Order No. S 117en, ISBN: 978-1-890841-37-9

Life with our Animal Brothers and Sisters
You, the Animal – You, the Human Being

An unusual book on animals that explains the emergence of the life forms of nature and the all-encompassing, effective and fundamental spiritual principles governing all of life. We learn about the communication between animals and nature beings, the possibility for people to communicate with animals, why animals attack us, the right way of treating them, and much more.

108 pages / Order No. S 133en, ISBN: 978-1-890841-25-6

NEW!

The Animal-Friendly Cookbook

Over the course of a lifetime, a person can save the lives of 450 animals, simply by not eating meat. This alone gives good reason to become vegetarian, or vegan! The bonus? You remain healthy and fit! This book is meant to serve all who want to contribute less and less to our world's environmental problems, to suffering in slaughterhouses and inhumane conditions in factory farming.

208 pages / High-gloss color illustr. / Order No. S 436en
ISBN: 978-1-890841-57-7

To order any of these books or to obtain a complete catalog of all our books, please contact:

THE WORD
P. O. Box 5643
97006 Wuerzburg
GERMANY

or:
Universal Life, the Inner Religion
P. O. Box 3549
Woodbridge, CT 06525
U S A
1-800-846-2691

or:
Universal Life, the Inner Religion
P. O. Box 55133
1800 Shepherd Ave., East
Toronto, ON M2J 5A0
CANADA
1-800-806-9997

www.universal-spirit.org
e-mail: info@universelles-leben.org

or:
Order our books at Amazon.com